Get ready for a refreshing journey! *Disciples of the Holy Spirit* is a call for the Church to revive her interest in the work and ministry of the Holy Spirit as vital to the discipleship process. George Kimber, writing with a pastor's heart and a professor's skill, thoughtfully explores how the fruit of the Spirit and the gifts of the Spirit must be viewed in a holistic way for believers to live empowered and Christ-like lives. You will find ample challenge and encouragement for both the charismatic and the non-charismatic. But don't be mistaken; this book is not simply a theological treatise. It is a call to live the Jesus-life through the empowering presence of the Holy Spirit. When you put this book down, you will have a deepening desire to live the Spirit-filled life!

> Dr. Craig Sider
> Executive Director, Center for Leadership Impact
> Former Bishop, Brethren in Christ Church (and delightfully, George Kimber's Bishop)

George Kimber's insights into the role of the Holy Spirit as discipling agent in the life of a disciple of Jesus Christ has the potential to revitalize the effectiveness of the discipleship event for pastor, church and individuals alike. George boldly articulates and then supports his assumption that we are to be "disciples of the Holy Spirit, directed by Christ."

As a believer and as a pastor I too have recognized that "we tend to manage the discipleship process" as George writes and this does indeed limit the effectiveness of the journey. George encourages the reader to let go of that management and return it to its rightful place, into the powerful and effective arms of the Holy Spirit. The result, according to George, will be a healthy and empowered church that is continuing the ministry of Jesus on earth as designed by her founder Jesus Christ.

In His book, George highlights Christian ethics as a beginning and necessary third, yet often missing, strand in the chord that is the manifestation of the Spirit's work in the church. His perspective is helpful for both the charismatic skeptic as well as the enthusiast. That three strand chord becomes balanced, strong and effective as Christian ethics, the fruits of the Spirit and the gifts of the Spirit are woven together.

George Kimber's holistic paradigm of every Christian becoming a "disciple of the Holy Spirit, directed by Christ," if embraced, has the potential of producing a relevant and vital church in the 21st century and beyond.

>Harry Jarrett, Jr.
>Lead Pastor, Neffsville Mennonite Church
>Lancaster, PA.

Disciples of the Holy Spirit

Continuing the Discipleship of Jesus Christ Through the Ministry of the Holy Spirit

Dr. George P. Kimber

To David with fond memories

George Kimber

CROSSBOOKS

CrossBooks™
A Division of LifeWay
1663 Liberty Drive
Bloomington, IN 47403
www.crossbooks.com
Phone: 1-866-879-0502

©2011 Dr. George P. Kimber. All rights reserved.

No part of this book may be reproduced, stored in a retrieval system, or transmitted by any means without the written permission of the author.

First published by CrossBooks 6/23/2011

ISBN: 978-1-6150-7929-2 (sc)
ISBN: 978-1-6150-7930-8 (hc)

Library of Congress Control Number: 2011932342

Printed in the United States of America

This book is printed on acid-free paper.

Cover picture by Matthew Durbin Ashland, Ohio

Because of the dynamic nature of the Internet, any web addresses or links contained in this book may have changed since publication and may no longer be valid. The views expressed in this work are solely those of the author and do not necessarily reflect the views of the publisher, and the publisher hereby disclaims any responsibility for them.

DEDICATION

To my dear friend and mentor, the late Dr. Nathaniel M. Van Cleave, who both taught and modeled the Spirit-filled life. To Dr. Arthur Climenhaga and the late Dr. Owen Alderfer, who were instrumental in securing my teaching position at Messiah College in Grantham, Pennsylvania, and who remained close friends for many years.

ACKNOWLEDGEMENTS

I am grateful to several people who encouraged and assisted me in the writing of this book: my wife, Kathleen, for her continuous encouragement and faith in me when I was experiencing setbacks and frequent computer problems; my dear daughter, Nan Shrigley, for her excellent editing of the text, offering both helpful suggestions and giving many hours of labor to help me bring this book into being; and my friends Mike Bennecoff and Pastor Joe Hyatt for their computer wisdom and help in my time of need.

CONTENTS

Dedication	v
Acknowledgements	vii
Foreword	xiii
Preface	xv
The Author's Journey as a Disciple of the Holy Spirit	xvii
Introduction	xix

CHAPTER ONE

WHO IS THE HOLY SPIRIT?	1
The Neglect and Confusion Concerning the Holy Spirit in Church History	1
The Development of the Doctrine of Cessationism Within the Scholarly Community.	3
The Abuses within the Pentecostal/Charismatic Movements and Non-Charismatic Groups within the Church	5
The Holy Spirit As a Person	6
The Holy Spirit and the Godhead	7

CHAPTER TWO

THE NEW TESTAMENT PATTERN OF HOLY SPIRIT DISCIPLESHIP	11
The Basic Understanding of Discipleship in the New Testament Culture	11
The Uniqueness of Discipleship under Jesus	12
The Importance Today for the Recognition of Discipleship through the Holy Spirit	13

CHAPTER THREE

JESUS, THE UNIQUE MODEL OF HOLY SPIRIT DISCIPLESHIP	19
The Purpose of Jesus Calling Disciples	20
The Incarnation, the Model of Perfect Discipleship	22

CHAPTER FOUR

THE ETHICAL FOUNDATION FOR DISCIPLES OF THE HOLY SPIRIT — 26
   The Ethics of Jesus as Seen in the Sermon on the Mount — 26
   The Ethics of Jesus Manifested in the Apostle Paul and Other Apostles — 32

CHAPTER FIVE

DISCIPLES OF THE HOLY SPIRIT: THE FRUIT DIMENSION — 40
   The Fruit Dimension in the Life of the Disciples (Galatians 5:16–26) — 40
   The Works of the Flesh Challenged by the Holy Spirit (Galatians 5:16–21, 24) — 41
   The Indwelling Spirit Develops and Produces Fruit in the Disciple (Galatians 5:22–23, 25, 26) — 42
   The Characteristics God Desires to See in the Disciple of the Holy Spirit (Galatians 5:22, 23) — 42
   Life in the Spirit expressed toward God: *Love, Joy, and Peace* — 43
   Life in the Spirit as expressed with others: *Patience, Kindness, and Goodness* — 46
   Life in the Spirit expressed in personal virtue: *Faithfulness, Meekness, and Self-Control* — 49

CHAPTER SIX

DISCIPLES OF THE HOLY SPIRIT: THE GIFTS DIMENSION — 54
   The Old Testament structure reflected in the New Testament — 54
   The Seven Motivational Gifts of Grace and their Functions (Romans 12:3–8) — 58
   The Office or Ministry Gifts of the Holy Spirit (Ephesians 4:11–16) — 71

CHAPTER SEVEN

THE MANIFESTING GIFTS OF THE HOLY SPIRIT (I Corinthians 12–14) — 79
   The Apostle Paul's Concern for the Corinthian Church — 79
   Three Guiding Principles which Determine a True Manifestation of the Holy Spirit (Corinthians 12:13) — 82
   Manifesting Gifts (I Corinthians 12:4–30) — 84

Three Major Categories: 85
　　The Need for a Full, Varied, and Multiple Manifestation of the
　　　Gifts of the Spirit 86
　　The Nine Manifesting Gifts (I Corinthians 12:8–10) 86
　　The Manifesting Gifts of Revelation 88
　　A Word of Wisdom *(Logos Sophias)* 88
　　A Word of Knowledge *(Logos Gnoseos)* 89
　　The Discerning of Spirits *(Diakrisies Pneumaton)* 89
　　The Manifesting Gifts of Power 90
　　The Manifestation of Faith *(Pistis)* 90
　　The Manifestation of the Working of Miracles *(Energemata
　　　Dunameon)* 91
　　Manifestation of the Gifts of Healing *(Charismata Lamaton)* 92
　　The Manifesting Gifts of Inspiration or the Voice of God 93
　　The Gift of Prophecy *(Propheteia)* 94
　　The Gift of Different Kinds of Tongues (I Corinthians 12:10) 97
　　The Gift of Interpretation of Tongues (I Corinthians 14:5, 13,
　　　27, 28) 103
　　Chart: The Holistic Work of the Holy Spirit 105

CHAPTER EIGHT

THE INTEGRATION OF THE FRUIT AND THE GIFTS OF THE HOLY SPIRIT 107

　　The Importance of Understanding the Church as the Body of
　　　Christ 108
　　The Results of the Integration of the Fruit and Gifts of the Holy
　　　Spirit 112

CHAPTER NINE

THE NEED FOR LOVE AS BEING THE *MODUS OPERANDI* IN ALL MANIFESTATIONS OF THE SPIRIT (I Corinthians 13:1–13) 114

　　The Absolute Necessity of Love to Everything Else (I
　　　Corinthians 13:1–3) 117
　　The Characteristics of Love (I Corinthians 13:4–6) 118
　　The Permanence of Love 121
　　The Importance of the Proper Regulation of Spiritual Gifts (I
　　　Corinthians 14:1–40) 123

CHAPTER TEN
DISCIPLES OF THE HOLY SPIRIT TODAY AND BEYOND   127
DISCUSSION QUESTIONS FOR EACH CHAPTER   131
RESOURCES   135

FOREWORD

Whether you are a newborn believer in Christ or an established leader or pastor with years of experience in serving Him, the book you have in hand may be one of the most important you will ever read. That is not a gratuitous encouragement to promote with fanfare the work of my friend, George Kimber, but the simple, unvarnished truth—timeless, healthy, fruit-bearing truth, presented by a proven, earnest, and faithful servant of the Savior. George and I first met decades ago when we were both students in college, preparing for the lifetime of ministry that is now very much "behind us." But with the joy of continued, effective labor still a privilege, we each enjoy our respective areas of services.

While commending him as a trusted minister of the Word of God, I also want to commend your wading into the spiritual waters of this volume for three reasons.

First, it is sound in its main focus. Discipleship—i.e., the equipping of people who *know* Christ to not only *grow* in Christ but also become ignited by God's Holy Spirit as they surrender to His empowering "fire" and thereby *glow* in Christ!

Second, it is timely in its appearance. There is a reawakening to the fact that "discipling" (Jesus' idea of growing "big people" enabled for ministry in their daily lives by His presence within them) is and always will be infinitely more fruitful and durable than "church growth strategies" (the human idea that "big churches" are essential to achieve what Jesus meant when He said, "I will build my Church."). Mega-churches are neither undesirable nor essential in Christ's purposes—especially if they keep the above "first priority" in focus.

Third, it squares with Christ's emphasis on the need that every one of us as believers has of becoming immersed in an ongoing relationship with the Holy Spirit.

"Being filled" with the Spirit is more than an encounter—it is a lifestyle. Becoming "equipped" as a believer is more than "knowing things about the Bible," but also involves "keeping on being filled with the Holy Spirit *daily*." It's by this means that He—the Holy Spirit Who "breathed" the Bible into being through human writers—can bring the Living Word to life and operational power as we discover Jesus' character and ministry dynamics "happening through us!"

Here is a handbook on individual and Church-wide health, geared to bring us into that multiplying love and grace that has always caused "the Church to be the Church!"

Jack W. Hayford
Chancellor, The King's College and Seminary
Founder, The Church on the Way
Los Angeles, California

PREFACE

The church periodically needs to return to the basic task of discipleship, due to the lack of discipline and commitment that takes place within the church. It is even more imperative when society lacks the same discipline and commitment to the important moral and spiritual values of life. The challenge is for each believer to recognize his or her position, in these last days, as a disciple of the Holy Spirit under the authority of Jesus Christ and His Word. This means assuming the responsibilities that accompany discipleship as it relates to the Christian lifestyle and ministry, so the church, as the body of Christ, may rise up as a model and a catalyst. The lack of discipline in the Church, especially in the North American context, is due partly to its pluralistic framework, which has taken its toll on the authority and witness of the Church to the larger society. With the resurgence of interest in recent charismatic revivals taking place in various parts of the world and the experiencing of the power and ministry of the Holy Spirit in our day, a clarion call for discipline and order must be heard. The charismatic movement, at large, has been problematic at times, due to its practitioners' lack of discipline in their worship style. Some of the unusual demonstrations that have taken place during their worship services call into question the way in which they bring glory to God and His character. When we give glory to God, we are expressing His dignity, His majesty, and His power. It seems to me that the fruit of the Spirit (Galatians 5:22, 23) that each believer possesses keeps to the forefront the ethical character of Jesus Christ in the midst of any manifestation associated with the ministry of the Holy Spirit. This is the premise and intent of this book. The book is not necessarily for scholarly discussion, but rather for pastors and congregations who may appreciate a practical, holistic understanding of the person and ministry of the Holy Spirit

THE AUTHOR'S JOURNEY AS A DISCIPLE OF THE HOLY SPIRIT

Before we embark on the content of this book, I think it would be appropriate to invite the readers to join the author in reflecting on his life's journey concerning the Holy Spirit. This book you are about to read constitutes my many years of experience and study of the person and work of the Holy Spirit in my life. Seldom do we have the opportunity to know an author's own experience of the truth he is communicating. Like most journeys, you will discover it is not a straight path. In my journey, much like John Bunyan's classic, **Pilgrim's Progress**, I experienced many curves, hills, and detours that brought at times discouragement, perplexity, misunderstandings, prejudices, and near defeat. It was God's intervention personally and through many of His caring servants that He afforded me His grace and courage to persevere. I discovered that by means of the indwelling of the Holy Spirit, I experienced love, joy, peace, and the assurance of God's abiding presence. However, I became aware that I not only needed God's presence, but I needed to know His Power and anointing for ministering the gospel.

Both my brother and I were raised to believe in God and have a reverential fear of Him through my dear mother, who insisted that the church would be of primary importance for her family. My father showed no interest in the church, but never interfered with my mother's wishes. Unfortunately, my father died early in life, leaving my widowed mother to maintain a home and build a future for herself and her two boys. My brother and I became actively engaged in the boys' choir, and later, I served as an acolyte in our church. The pastor, Rev. Chafe, became a surrogate spiritual father to me. As I served beside him, I learned to respect and to love the ways of the church. My mother's fondest wish was that someday I would become an Episcopal pastor. However, I had my own idea of what I wanted to be and do in life.

Having failed to complete my high school education, I joined the Navy. It was wartime, and I was much too young and inexperienced to be aware of the dangers. However, I learned some of the hard ways of life that would prepare me to later come alongside others who themselves were dealing with serious life issues and perplexed about their futures. God and the church were pretty much absent from my life during this time in the service. Following my discharge, I eventually married and came under the influence of a caring, godly father and mother-in-law. Observing their walk of faith, I discovered that my early religious experience had been more church-ianity and not true Christianity. One Sunday in 1949, while attending a worship service at a Foursquare Gospel Church with my wife and in-laws, I encountered, for the first time, the presence and power of the Holy Spirit entering my heart, and I received Christ as my personal Savior. After some time, I experienced the empowerment of the Holy Spirit and a definite call into the ministry. After receiving Biblical training, I was licensed and ordained with the International Church of the Foursquare Gospel. In the following twenty years, my ministry included serving as an evangelist and church planting both in Illinois and California. In 1962, I felt the call to teach and began pursuing degree programs in several seminaries. Meanwhile, the Foursquare denomination invited me to teach in their Bible College in Mount Vernon, Ohio, where I taught until 1968. I continued pursuing my studies at Ashland Theological Seminary in Ashland, Ohio. Upon completing my MDiv in 1969, I was called to teach at Messiah College in Pennsylvania, which extended to twenty-two years. During that time, I secured additional degrees at Ashland Theological Seminary an M.A. (1975) and a DMin (1979). I retired from Messiah College in 1992, but continuing ministry, I planted a church in Pennsylvania and pastored it until retiring in 2000. As of June 2009, I continue to serve within local congregations, teaching and occasionally taking conference assignments and other speaking engagements.

INTRODUCTION

Without a doubt, the Church must continually revive its interest in the gifts and operation of the Holy Spirit to each generation. There is renewed interest in the area of the supernatural today that is both exciting and frightening. I am apprehensive about the many expressions of the mystical that are in the forefront today. We have been invaded by many occult movements and the unusual acceptance of the Eastern religions, along with the popularization of the so-called New Age movement. In addition to these, we have increased interest in the psychic use of the media of television promoted by popular figures of the entertainment world. There is great interest in angels who supposedly bring us secret knowledge and power, guide us into the way of blessing and prosperity, and give their protection. The attraction to these areas gives evidence of society's feeling of helplessness and frustration as people seek security and success, longing for purpose and meaning to their existence.

Augustine's historic statement of the fourth century, "We are restless until we find our rest in Thee," is still an appropriate and valid truth to be considered today. It's a sad commentary, but society is not readily drawn to the church when seeking meaning and help outside of itself. Is it not strange that the greatest depository of truth, the Scriptures, that contain the meaning of life and life more abundantly, is passed by or ignored? We can continue to rationalize and blame it on humanity's sinfulness and Satan's deception which certainly are part of the problem but is that the whole problem? The Church needs to take inventory as to how it is proclaiming the gospel of Jesus Christ and is demonstrating the work of the Holy Spirit through individual lives and the collective body of Christ.

There are two major areas where the church seems to fail to communicate with clarity the character and ministry of the Holy Spirit as expressed by the fruit of the Spirit (Galatians 5:23) and the gifts of the Spirit (I Corinthians 12–14). The basic problem is that these areas are frequently separated from each other, rather than being viewed together in a holistic way. It is my contention that it is imperative for these two areas to be integrated; otherwise, we distort the purpose of the incarnation of Jesus Christ. The main purpose of His incarnation was, first of all, to reveal to us what God is like in His ethical character. This is revealed to us through the fruit of the Holy Spirit. Secondly, the incarnation was to demonstrate what God could do by His omnipotence (power) and sovereignty. This is revealed to us through the gifts of the Holy Spirit.

Consider with me for a moment a wonderful and remarkable truth which I do not think has been apprehended or understood by much of the Church. Consider how this incarnation purpose is thus transferred to His Church, which is aptly referred to as His body (Colossians 1:24). What are the implications of this title given to the church? First of all, it is the work of the Holy Spirit to baptize us into the body of Christ individually; thereafter, we become members one with another (I Corinthians 12:12–27). Secondly, this corporate body has Christ as its head and authority (Ephesians 5:23). Thus, Christ directing the church, His body, through the Holy Spirit determines to have the church reveal what God is like in His character (the fruit of the Spirit, Galatians 5:22, 23) and what God can do (represented by the gifts of the Spirit, Romans 12:3–8; Ephesians 4:7–13; I Corinthians 12, 13, 14). The final implication is that with Christ as the head and we His body, the Holy Spirit, having baptized us into the body, now indwells all its members. We are, then, disciples of the Holy Spirit, directed by Christ to accomplish His will and purpose. It may appear to be a radical concept in referring to believers as disciples of the Holy Spirit rather than disciples of Christ; however, this is not an attempt to make a contradistinction between Christ and the Holy Spirit. Rather, it is suggesting the integration between the discipleship of Jesus, mediated primarily through the Word of God, and the Holy Spirit, mediated through the direct communication with the believer. Neither is there an attempt to divide the Trinity or elevate the Holy Spirit above the Father and Son, but rather distinguish the particular function of the

Holy Spirit in the Godhead as it applies to the believer and the Church, His body. There is certainly no competition or jealousy in the Godhead, since each part functions as one essence to accomplish the ultimate plan of God. It is a dynamic thought that recognizes and affirms the *authority* of the Spirit in discipleship by emphasizing the initiative and direction of the Holy Spirit in the process.

Apart from the authority of the Spirit and our cooperation with Him, we tend to "manage" the process of discipleship by ourselves and limit its effectiveness. I believe this is a needed corrective for those who tend make discipleship the product of a well-organized methodology initiated by the church. The concept of the discipleship of the Holy Spirit restores and enlarges the sovereignty and initiative of the Godhead in discipleship. This is not to discredit the "disciplines" as promoted by several authors, such as Richard Foster in **Celebration of Discipline** and Dallas Willard in **The Spirit of the Disciplines**. These writers certainly recognized the work of the Holy Spirit in the process, but unfortunately, some interpret these disciplines as developing mental or habitual practices. There are two sides of Christianity: the *outward,* consisting of the work of Jesus Christ His ministry, death, resurrection, and ascension; and the *inward* side, represented by the operation of the Holy Spirit through whom the reality of these facts are revealed to us. The Holy Spirit is sent to do *in* us what Christ has done *for* us. Oswald Chambers, in **My Utmost for the Highest***,* reflected, "when I commit myself to the revelation made in the New Testament, I receive from God the gift of the Holy Spirit who begins to interpret to me what Jesus did; and does in me subjectively all that Jesus did for me objectively. Jesus alluded to this when He told His disciples in **John 14:12**, 'I tell you the truth, anyone who has faith in me will do what I have been doing. He will do even greater things than these, because I am going to the Father'" **(20)**.

No doubt Jesus is answering the disciples' questioning minds as to what their role would be if He is going away. This was another word of comfort to them, in that his going away would not end the work that he had begun. Notice that the promise would be fulfilled "because I go to my Father." Once Jesus ascended to the Father, the Holy Spirit descended and indwells His disciples. What does it mean that they will do even greater things? Simply this: the ministry and the character of Christ would be demonstrated through them in unlimited measure and larger in scope. The ministry of Christ was limited in scope, due to His physical presence. However, now since His ascension, He indwells His disciples by the Holy Spirit, and His work now flows to the ends of the earth through them. They could now ask God for anything pertaining to His will and purpose, and it will be done. We need to grasp this truth today for ourselves—that we are His disciples and are also indwelt by the Holy Spirit with this same promise that was given to the early disciples. That's why I do not hesitate to refer to us as disciples of the Holy Spirit, who enables us to glorify Jesus in word and deed. I remember singing a song years ago: "Every promise in the book is mine, every chapter, every verse, every line, I am living in His love divine, every promise in the book is mine."(author Rick Altizer) There is a great need for us to bring ourselves into these promises and believe them today.

It is unfortunate that in some circles of Christianity, there is a tendency to relegate some of the promises of the Scriptures only relevant to past generations and not applicable to the present. God's covenant with Abraham and his descendants was not just for the rest of the Old Testament, but the whole New Testament. The covenant included a reference to "all the families of the earth" (Genesis 12:1–3; 17:7). Only now in Christ have these promises begun to be fulfilled, for Jesus Christ and His people are the true seed of Abraham (Galatians 3:29). The final fulfillment lies beyond history. Then Abraham's seed will be a great multitude that no one can count, and their inheritance will be the New Jerusalem (Genesis 22:17; Hebrews 11:8–12, 16, 39, 40; Revelation 7:9). The Church today, in its contemporary mold, has made great strides in drawing huge numbers of people by the use of technology and entertainment. We are succeeding in gathering crowds into our beautiful and expensive church buildings on Sunday and developing programs to attract more and more people. We have allowed the culture to dictate our agenda and created so-called "seeker-sensitive" programs to assure people they will not be forced to be uncomfortable. We end up with the majority of church members as simply spectators and not many being converted and discipled. I agree with John MacArthur in his book **Hard to Believe: "It's Christianity for consumers: Christianity Lite, the redirection, watering down, and misinterpretation of the biblical gospel in an attempt to make it more palatable and popular.**

It tastes great going down and settles light" (p.2). It is my contention that, in these last days, Jesus is more fervently calling us to "make disciples and teach them to obey my commands" (Matthew 28:18). My desire is to challenge the Church to rethink its view of the Holy Spirit, His ministry to the church, and His gifts and allow them to operate without fear of fanaticism, based upon the virtues of the fruit of the Spirit to govern the results. We need to be disciples of the Holy Spirit today as ordained by Christ, just as He ordained his disciples after His ascension. My goal is to give a holistic understanding of the work of the Holy Spirit that dispels fear of His ministry caused by misunderstanding.

Chapter One

WHO IS THE HOLY SPIRIT?

What word association do you make with "Holy Spirit?" Speaking in tongues? Sanctification? Pentecostalism? Prophecy? Charismatics? Mystical? Spiritual? Inspiration of Scriptures? Emotionalism? Fanaticism? Bizarre actions? Such diverse associations show why we have difficulty understanding the person, character, and ministry of the Holy Spirit. Why do Christians continually reject and debate about the Holy Spirit? Many questions expressed within the Body of Christ continue to cry out for answers. In my years of ministry, preaching, and teaching within both the Pentecostal and non-Pentecostal communities, I have encountered numerous questions and opinions concerning the Holy Spirit. A number of factors create confusion and perplexity concerning the person and ministry of the Holy Spirit. Let me briefly address some of these major issues.

The Neglect and Confusion Concerning the Holy Spirit in Church History

Throughout the greater part of church history, one of the most neglected and distorted doctrines is the biblical teaching concerning the Holy Spirit. Historically, the Holy Spirit has been classified within the larger framework of the Trinity. In order to maintain the belief in one God (monotheism), some, having stressed the unity of the Trinity, have denied that there were three distinct persons in the Godhead. The Jews believe that there is only one God, and this God is Yahweh, the God of Abraham, Isaac, and Jacob. The first Christians were Jewish converts and still affirmed their belief in one God. Though they recognized God the Father and the person of Jesus Christ, who introduced the work of the Holy Spirit, they wondered how they could confess one God in three persons and still be monotheistic. That is, how can God be known as Father, Son, and Spirit, as one being, yet each person distinct from the other? The early believers were careful about making an issue about the Trinity, lest it be misunderstood as promoting three gods in the polytheistic Roman culture in which they lived. Romans typically believed in many gods; they simply would have added the Trinity of Christianity to their display of gods in their pantheon.

In the third century, some attempted to solve the problem by picturing God appearing first as the Father, then further on in history appearing as the Son, and finally appearing as the Holy Spirit. Most Christians don't have difficulty in relating to the Father and the Son, because of their experiences with human fathers and sons presented to us in physical bodies. When it comes to the Holy Spirit, however, we think in non-personal terms and refer to Him as "it." This makes it difficult to conjure up an image from something invisible. The King James Version of the Bible does not help us when it refers to the Holy Spirit as the *Holy Ghost*. I heard of a Sunday school teacher who was trying to portray the reality of the Holy Spirit to a group of children by blowing on a piece of paper and letting it "fly away." She was pointing out to the children that the Spirit is like that; it is like the wind, and even though the wind is invisible, we know it is real. At that moment, a six-year boy blurted out, "But I want the wind to be un-invisible!" How often we feel like that. We want a personal, tangible reference.

In AD 325, the Council of Nicea convened as the result of a bishop by the name of Arius who proposed that while Jesus is highly exalted as the greatest creation of the one true God and worthy of honor, he should not be seen as God himself. A number of Arians at the council fervently argued this position. But another bishop by the name of Athanasius, who was a gifted, godly theologian, defended the deity of Christ against Arius's view. Athanasius argued that the New Testament clearly revealed Christ's deity and that He was of the very same nature as the Father. Athanasius prevailed, and the Nicene Creed was written. This creed continues to be recited today in many of our churches. This creed went through much discussion in later councils, but it is not our purpose to explore all of the ramifications that took place.

The original Nicene Creed of AD 325 went as follows: **"We believe in one God the Father All-sovereign, maker of all things visible and Invisible; And in one Lord Jesus Christ, the Son of God, begotten of the Father, only-begotten, that is, of the substance of the Father, God of God, Light of Light, true God of true God, begotten not made, of one substance with the Father, through whom all things were made, things in heaven and things on earth; who for us men and for our salvation came down and was made flesh, and became man, suffered, and rose on the third day, ascended into the heavens, is coming to judge living and dead. And in the Holy Spirit"** (Henry Betterson, *Documents of the Christian Church*, 35).

Notice how the creed abruptly ended with simply mentioning **"And in the Holy Spirit."** There were further statements mentioned in the later revisions of the creed, but not as definitive as the Father and the Son. No councils ever convened to discuss the person of the Holy Spirit, therefore resulting in a vague understanding of this third person of the trinity as a force or influence.

The Development of the Doctrine of Cessationism Within the Scholarly Community.

Cessationists consist of Christians, some of whom are scholars, who believe that the gifts of the Holy Spirit have ceased to exist. They maintain that the manifestation of the gifts died out with the twelve apostles and the completion of the Canon of Scripture. It was Benjamin Warfield, a professor at Princeton Seminary, who popularized the argument that the miraculous gifts of the Spirit were given only to a few, and the purpose of these gifts was to authenticate the apostles. However, when the apostles died, the gifts ceased, and with the completion of the Bible, the gifts were not needed. These arguments have spread even today to our modern theological descendants and have caused undue skepticism among the church. The following is the primary passage used to support their argument: "**Love never fails. But where there are prophecies, they will cease; where there are tongues, they will be stilled; where there is knowledge, it will pass away. For we know in part and we prophesy in part but when perfection comes, the imperfect disappears. When I was a child, I talked like a child, I thought like a child, I reasoned like a child. When I became a man, I put childish ways behind me. Now we see through a poor reflection as in a mirror; then we shall see face to face. Now I know in part; then I shall know fully, even as I am fully known**" (I Corinthians 13:8–12).

The statement in verse 10, **"when perfection comes,"** is believed to be the completion of the Bible. It appears to me that the context refers to our perfection, not the completion of the Bible. The context talks about "we" and "I" knowing in part, then knowing fully; being a child, then growing into a man. Some interpret the perfection as the eternal age when all earthly things cease and we will experience eternal perfection. This is inferred in verse 8, where "prophecies," "tongues," and "knowledge" will cease and give way to the perfect, heavenly realm. In other words, spiritual gifts will not cease until Christ returns. Paul told the Corinthians, "You do not lack any spiritual gift as you eagerly wait for our Lord Jesus Christ to be revealed" (I Corinthians 1:7). Paul is saying that they will find gifts valuable until Christ returns.

The other question is, "Did miraculous gifts cease with the apostles?" When we turn to the book of Acts, we discover that various gifts of the Holy Spirit are being exercised. We discover many people who spoke in tongues, and many received the gift of prophecy. Jack Deer, in his book ***Surprise by the Power of the Spirit*** (Zondervan, 1993, 234), gives the following list of such incidents:

Those who spoke in tongues:

1. The 120 (Acts 2)
2. The Samaritans (They almost certainly spoke in tongues, for Acts 8:18 says that Simon "saw" the Samaritans receiving the Holy Spirit.)
3. Cornelius and the Gentiles with him (Acts 10:45–46)
4. The twelve disciples at Ephesus (Acts 19:6)

Those who received the gift of prophecy:

1. The prophet Agabus (Acts 11:28; 21:10–11)
2. The individuals in Acts 13:1
3. The prophets Judas and Silas (Acts 15:32)
4. The disciples of Tyre who "though the Spirit" urged Paul not to go on to Jerusalem (Acts 21:4)
5. Philip's four unmarried daughters who prophesied (Acts 21:9)
6. Ananias (Acts 9:10–18)

The Abuses within the Pentecostal/Charismatic Movements and Non-Charismatic Groups within the Church

Those who have received the empowerment of the Spirit generally display great enthusiasm and emotion, which is interpreted by many as undue fanaticism. I would like to point out that there is a healthy enthusiasm that accompanies any experience received from God. The Holy Spirit alone can create a healthy enthusiasm without the human factor. We must let God work and let the human agent walk softly before Him, watching, waiting, and praying. It is important to build our experience on the Word of God. I remember my pastor saying years ago, "For every counterfeit, there is an original." Satan counterfeits the things of God. He has never come up with an original idea of his own.

There have been many abuses within the Christian community that have created embarrassment to the mission and purpose of God. Many of these abuses were the result of overzealous individuals; because a lack of knowledge of God's Word; or a person seeking to gain notoriety, power, and influence. Among the various denominations, the Pentecostal and charismatic groups have been singled out as the most abusive concerning the ministry and work of the Holy Spirit among them. Their unusual demonstrations and enthusiasm has, for the most part, been viewed as fanaticism and faulty theology. However, theological or doctrinal abuses concerning the Holy Spirit have not been confined to classic Pentecostals or the contemporary charismatic movements. There are abuses and disagreements among non-charismatics in the Church at large that resulted in additional confusion concerning the character and work of the Holy Spirit.

The problem is that they do not distinguish between people and doctrine. There is little recognition of the areas of doctrinal agreement and focus on behavior. Personal behavior will differ in most movements, to their embarrassment. In my pursuit of ministry, I personally experienced the prejudice and lack of love and grace exhibited to me because of my charismatic beliefs that extended beyond their experience, yet my basic doctrinal position was in line with their evangelical faith. It is not my intent to explore and discuss or argue these differences. The purpose of this book is to consider chiefly what the Scriptures have to reveal concerning the Holy Spirit. If we indeed are to be disciples of the Holy Spirit, it is important we not only know about Him, but also to know Him intimately. Knowing God has to do with relationship. Jesus said, **"If you love me, you will obey what I command. And I will ask the Father, and he will give you another Counselor to be with you forever the Spirit of truth. The world cannot accept him, because it neither sees him nor knows him. But you know him, for he lives with you and will be in you"** (**John 14:15–17**). Let us then proceed to see how the Scriptures unfold in describing Him:

The Holy Spirit As a Person

One of the most difficult aspects in understanding the Godhead is recognizing the Holy Spirit as a person. Because He is a person and we are also persons, we can know Him and be His disciples, learning how to obey and live the commands of Jesus. There have been those who have denied the personality of the Spirit in one form or another. Many preachers and theologians refer to the Spirit as an "it" and not a "he." He has been considered a created, impersonal influence or power, but not recognized as the third person of the Trinity. The Scriptures give a number of images attributed to the Holy Spirit that cause many difficulty in identifying him as a person, images such as "**dove**," "**wind**," "**fire**," "**oil**," and "**water**." The Holy Spirit is a divine, personal being, with all the qualities, characteristics, and attributes of personality. Consider just a few:

Personal Pronouns found In John's gospel: **"He will testify of me"** (John 15:26); **"I will send *Him* unto you"** (John 16:7); **"He will not speak of His own"** (John. 16:13); **and "He will bring glory to me"** (John 16:14). As we look further in Scripture, we find:

Personal Characteristics ascribed to Him. The Holy Spirit has all the qualities of personality. He has intelligence (Romans 8:27), power of volition or choice (I Corinthians 12:11), and knowledge (I Corinthians 2:10–11). We find further that:

Personal Acts are ascribed to Him. He teaches (Luke 12:12; John 14:26; I Corinthians 2:13); He regenerates, quickens, and gives spiritual birth (John 3:5, 6, 8); He fills believers (Acts 2:4, 8; 7:55); He guides (Matthew 4:1; John 16:13; Galatians 5:18); He comforts (John 14:16–17; Ephesians 2:18); He dwells among and within believers (I Corinthians 3:16; Romans 8:11; II Timothy 1:14); He makes intercession for the saints (Romans 8:26, 27); and He strengthens believers (Ephesians 3:16).

Lastly, He is **Affected as a Person.** He may be grieved (Ephesians 4:30), resisted (Acts 7:51), lied to (Acts 5:3), quenched (I Thessalonians 5:19), and blasphemed against (Matthew 12:31, 32). In the light of such evidence from Scripture, how could anyone deny that the Holy Spirit is a person?

The Holy Spirit and the Godhead

Gordon Fee, in his book ***Paul, the Spirit, and the People of God***, states, **"The Spirit must be reinstated into the Trinity, where he has never been excluded in our creeds and liturgies, but has been practically excluded from the experienced life of the church"** (45).

There has been much discussion and debate concerning the Trinity (Father, Son, and Holy Spirit) and their relationship to each other. My concern is that there is an apparent separation that some infer concerning the relationship of the Holy Spirit to the Father and Christ as to His deity. It is important that we distinguish the role and work of the Spirit in connection to His person. In focusing only upon the work of the Holy Spirit, we tend to see Him only an agent of the Father and the Son but with no equality with them. We must understand His position in the Trinity as co-equal and working together with the Father and the Son to accomplish their eternal purpose. The doctrine of the Trinity is necessary for producing our Christian faith. Some years ago, I became aware of the importance of the unified work of the Father, Son, and Holy Spirit to the Christian faith. My discovery was affirmed when I read Bruce A. Ware's book, **Father, Son, and Holy Spirit,** in which he stated, "The doctrine of the Trinity is both central and necessary for the Christian faith to be what it is. Remove the Trinity, and the whole Christian faith disintegrates. it becomes clear that the work of God (e.g., creation, redemption, and consummation) can be rightly understood only as the work of the Father, Son and Holy Spirit unified in the purpose of the work but distinct in the participation and contribution of each member" (16–17).

To illustrate this truth, I would like you to consider the following diagrams:

THE DIVINE GODHEAD

	Function	*Purpose*
	FATHER—Decrees the Plan	
ONE ESSENCE	THE SON—Provides the Means	REDEMPTION
	THE HOLY SPIRIT—Executes Plan	

The Scriptures clearly reveal the Trinity, even though our rational minds cannot fully comprehend it. An important point is that even though we observe God functioning in three persons, we also recognize the unity between them to accomplish an eternal purpose. They form one essence, but they also are disclosed to us as Father, Son, and Holy Spirit. These constitute functional terms for God's purposes to be carried out and understood by us. You will notice that they function in different ways to bring about the salvation and redemption for the human race. Notice how this paradigm coincides with God's plan for marriage and family:

MARRIAGE AND FAMILY

	Function	Purpose
	MAN—Husband, Father: Provider	
ONE FLESH	WOMAN—Wife, Mother: Nurturer	FAMILY
	CHILDREN—result of "one flesh" union and focus of parent's love	

Since man and woman were created in God's image, He declared they would be joined together as "one flesh" patterned after the Godhead principle. The only way man and woman could experience and demonstrate what it means to be "one essence" like God is within the marriage covenant and the physical act of intercourse. Contrary to modern thinking, this act is not merely for pleasure or to satisfy a biological need for gratification (I Corinthians 6:12–15). Actually, intercourse is more metaphysical than physical. In the bond of coming together in covenant of love, there is physical, emotional, and spiritual fervor taking place to a point of desiring to be consumed by each other. As "one flesh," the man and woman are in the sight of God, and hopefully to each other, co-equal, and in a sense, co-eternal. However, for the sake of producing family, they assume the functions of husband and wife, father and mother. Out of this type of being comes a separate entity. Now the parents, seeing their oneness in this child in a genetic, emotional, and spiritual way, begin to function as one with the child. As a result, the child receives love, protection, nurture, and guidance as a result. This is God's plan for producing family and a healthy generation. Some of the most horrible crimes in our present society and world are demonstrated in abortions, incest, child abuse, divorces, and just plain self-indulgence. The reducing of marriage to sex and merely fulfilling the biological urge is pure blasphemy to the Creator and His purpose. Because sex is divorced from covenant love to God and to one another, when a child is born, the result is that the child is generally unwanted. The child becomes a burden and causes irritation and frustration. The baby becomes a hindrance to the couple's freedom, pleasures, and desires. The result is child abuse and neglect! What a difference this would make in our society today if this concept was understood and embraced by not only Christian married couples, but also by non-Christians.

The third paradigm demonstrates how the Trinity pattern applies the Church:

THE CHURCH

	Function	*Purpose*
	CHRIST—The head and authority	(Present)
ONE BODY	HOLY SPIRIT—Indwelling believers	KINGDOM OF GOD
	DISCIPLES OF HOLY SPIRIT—Empowered with Spiritual Gifts	(Future/Eternal)

The presence of Christ is now operative through His Church, which is designated as His body. The image of the Church as a body is significant to our understanding of its function. The apostle Paul uses this imagery as he rehearses the functions of the spiritual gifts in I Corinthians 12:12–27 and refers to the body as a unit—though it is made up of many parts, **it forms one body**. Each member has been baptized in the body by the Holy Spirit and His indwelling them and distributing His gifts to them under the headship and authority of Christ. This pattern creates the present kingdom of God on earth and establishes the future, eternal kingdom in heaven. It is obvious that if this pattern was understood by the Church today, with its multiple denominations and structures, the kingdom of God would be realized more readily and would result in greater unity and purpose to the world. Christ stated God's desire for His disciples in John 17:11: **"That they may be one as we are one."** The reality of this oneness will be realized at the second coming of Christ, when all believers will be taken to heaven as one Church, established in the kingdom of God. Having established the identity of the Holy Spirit, it is imperative that we discuss the identity and meaning of discipleship as it relates to the ministry of the Holy Spirit within the believer.

Chapter Two

THE NEW TESTAMENT PATTERN OF HOLY SPIRIT DISCIPLESHIP

As believers, we are often inclined to think of discipleship only in terms of the disciples of Jesus Christ and confine its significance to the time of the Gospels for that particular time and purpose. I would prefer to conceptualize discipleship along a historical continuum to our present day, initiated by Christ Himself and carried on by the person of the Holy Spirit within us.

The Basic Understanding of Discipleship in the New Testament Culture

To understand more clearly the need for the church to be a discipling body with the help of the Holy Spirit, let's rehearse, briefly, the New Testament pattern of discipleship. The Greek word **mathetes (pronounced mar-thay-tase**—disciple) comes from the verb *manthano* (to learn). Thus, a disciple is a learner, or one who comes under the discipline of another namely, a teacher. However, the etymology of a word, though important, is not sufficient to make a precise connection between the idea of disciple and learner. We must observe how it is used in its cultural setting. The word *mathetes* is used in a variety of ways in the Gospels. First, it is applied to the twelve whom Jesus chose to be with Him. They were chosen in order that He might train them to both teach and serve (Mark 3:14). They responded to Jesus as committed disciples, surrendering everything to live in obedience to Him. These are the conditions expressed by Jesus in Luke 14:26: *"If anyone comes to me and does not hate his father and mother, his wife and children, his brothers and sisters—yes, even his own life—he cannot be my disciple."* Secondly, **mathetes** identifies followers of various schools or traditions. A **mathetes** was one who attached himself to another to gain some practical or theoretical knowledge, whether by instruction or experience. In the Greek culture, many of the philosophers like Socrates, Plato, and others—were sought out by such persons. There were also those who were followers of schools of thought such as the popular philosophies of Stoicism and Epicureanism.

Thirdly, in the time of Jesus, there were those who considered themselves disciples of the Pharisees (Matthew 22:16; Mark 2:18; Luke 5:33) and others who considered themselves disciples of John the Baptist (Matthew 11:2; Mark 2:18; Luke 5:33; John 1:35–36). These do not necessarily identify in the traditional teacher-learner relationship, but rather as persons who are adherents of a movement.

The Uniqueness of Discipleship under Jesus

What, then, makes discipleship under Jesus different or unique? When we are called to follow Christ, we are not simply adherents to His teaching, but summoned to an exclusive attachment to His person. Dietrich Bonhoeffer in **The Cost of Discipleship** puts it very well as he writes, *"Discipleship means adherence to Christ, and because Christ is the object of that adherence, it must take the form of discipleship. An abstract Christology, a doctrinal system, a general religious knowledge on the subject of grace or on the forgiveness of sins, render discipleship superfluous, and in fact they positively exclude any idea of discipleship whatever, and are essentially inimical to the whole conception of following Christ. With an abstract idea it is possible to enter into a relation of formal knowledge, to become enthusiastic about it, and perhaps even to put it into practice; but it can never be followed in personal obedience" (63).*

After the Resurrection, Jesus charged His followers to *"go and make disciples of all nations" (Matthew 28:19)*. The mandate was not to win adherents for a movement; rather, the disciples were to teach those who believed to obey everything He had commanded them (**Matthew 28:20**).

The Importance Today for the Recognition of Discipleship through the Holy Spirit

The church today needs to recognize and put into practice the discipleship ordained through the indwelling and power of the Holy Spirit, mainly that of instruction and discipline. I am particularly concerned about the general attitude that has prevailed both in the traditional Pentecostal and contemporary charismatic movements relative to discipleship. They have, I believe unintentionally, created a dichotomy of one type of discipleship under Jesus Christ and another under the Holy Spirit. Though this dichotomy is not articulated in doctrinal statements, it is evident in attitude and practice. For example, it is not unusual to observe those supposedly "ministering in the power of the Spirit" to leave the impression that any kind of behavior is acceptable under this rubric. Many somewhat bizarre happenings are legitimatized without being challenged or investigated. Thus, such demonstrations and expressions become offensive, demeaning, and unprofitable to the kingdom of God. R. Hollis Grause, in discussing **"Issues in Pentecostalism"** in *Perspectives on the New Pentecostalism* , speaking to the issue of using emotional experience as a basis for our critiques, says, **"it is assumed that the Holy Spirit (as understood emotionally and experientially) confirms as good whatever one is and whatever one does when he is being 'blessed.' This is a shallow form of emotional pragmatism that is passed off as the guidance of the Holy Spirit"** (115).

While serving as pastor of a Pentecostal church in California, I encountered situations where certain individuals would exercise their spiritual gifts in our worship service. Unfortunately, my knowledge and understanding of the gifts of the Holy Spirit were still being studied and developed. It would frustrate me to know how to deal with the legitimacy and still maintain a sense of order in the worship service. This was compounded by the fact that these persons were not members of our church and only visited from time to time. Most of the time, the exercise of their so-called gifts was expressed in the form of prophecy or a message in tongues, followed by an interpretation. The congregation developed mixed feelings about them, since for the most part, these people were unknown to us. We did not want to reject this if truly it was a manifestation from God. The congregation looked to me for direction and understanding. This prompted me to do more intensive study of the Holy Spirit in the life of the believer and the Church. On one particular occasion, after a woman stood up during my sermon and proceeded to speak in tongues and quickly gave an interpretation, I decided to invite her to my office following the service. As I questioned her about her demonstration, she became indignant. In her opinion, I had no right to challenge or question the manifestation of the Holy Spirit. This woman could not even tell me where these gifts were found in Scripture, nor could she explain their purpose, except that God gave her a message. She further told me she was never instructed from the Scriptures on these matters and that she simply received these gifts during a revival service. She sincerely thought that God had ordained her to travel around to various churches and exercise her gifts. I offered to mentor her, and she accepted the invitation. To the joy of both of us, she developed a wholesome understanding of her gifts and how to exercise them properly.

First of all, no one ever questioned her exercising of the gifts, because it was presumed it would be "quenching the Spirit." Secondly, there was no instruction offered to her; again, because it was presumed that one cannot give instruction in what the Holy Spirit is doing. Thirdly, because she did not understand the purpose and meaning of these gifts, people were confused and questioned what God was trying to do. As a disciple of Jesus Christ, she should have understood that she was also a disciple of the Holy Spirit, including His fruit as well as His gifts, under the authority of Jesus Christ, and there should be no dichotomy, but integration. Discipleship includes both the fruit of the Spirit and the gifts of the Spirit—that is, a demonstration in believers' lives of Christ's character and His power in the world. When the apostle Paul wrote to the church in Corinth, he did not hesitate to challenge the operation of the gifts in the church, because he knew they needed instruction and discipline. When Jesus called His first disciples to instruct them, He was present with them in the flesh. They heard His teaching and responded to His authoritative command,

"Follow me!" They seem to have had an advantage over us today. Now Christ has ascended into heaven, and we can see Him no more until He returns at the end of the age. How can we respond, since we do not have the same advantage of the early disciples? Surely Christ has provided a way for us. Yes, He did through the inspired Word of God and the Holy Spirit, which has been given to us. **"All this I have spoken while still with you. But the Counselor, the Holy Spirit, whom the Father will send in my name, will teach you all things and will remind you of everything I have said to you" (John 14:25, 26).** One of the great prayers in the Bible is in John 17, where Jesus prays for Himself, His disciples, and all future believers: **"My prayer is not for them alone, I pray also for those who will believe in me through their message, that all of them may be one, Father, just as you are in me and I am in you. May they also be in us so that the world may believe that you sent me. I give them the glory that you gave me, that they may be one as we are one: I in them and you in me" (John 17:20–23).**

One should never conclude that we have less understanding today than those early disciples. In fact, we have a greater advantage and privilege because of the indwelling of the Holy Spirit and a completed Canon of Scripture from Genesis to Revelation. The early disciples of Jesus became aware of the ministry of the Holy Spirit in their master's life, and in turn, under His direction, they began to experience the same power in their own lives and ministry. As they witnessed His miraculous works and heard His teaching of the kingdom, they too became agents in advancing the kingdom (Luke 10:1–24).

Before Christ ascended into heaven, He desired that they receive the fullness of the Holy Spirit (Luke 24:45–49) so they could continue as His disciples under the Holy Spirit's administration. A number of passages in Scripture allude to this, but let me call your attention to a number of prominent passages that reflect this truth—namely, *Acts 1:1, 2 (NIV): "In my former book, Theophilus, I wrote about all Jesus began to do and teach until the day he was taken up to heaven, after giving instructions through the Holy Spirit to the apostles he had chosen."* Note that this states that Jesus, though ascended, was still giving instructions to His disciples (apostles) "through the Holy Spirit."

In Acts 10:19, Peter was directed to the house of Cornelius: *"While Peter was thinking about the vision, the Spirit said to him, 'Simon, three men are looking for you. So get up and go downstairs. Do not hesitate to go with them, for I have sent them.'"* In Acts 13:2, 4, Barnabas and Saul were sent forth: *"While they were worshiping the Lord and fasting, the Holy Spirit said, 'Set apart for me Barnabas and Saul for the work to which I have called them' …. The two of them, sent on their way by the Holy Spirit."* In Acts 15:28, at the council in Jerusalem, *"It seemed good to the Holy Spirit and to us not to burden you with anything beyond the following requirements."* In Acts 20:22, 23, Paul was compelled to go to Jerusalem: *"And now, compelled by the Holy Spirit, I am going to Jerusalem, not knowing what will happen to me there. I only know that in every city the Holy Spirit warns me that prison and hardships are facing me."*

Throughout Luke's gospel, he emphasizes the work of the Holy Spirit. The number of references to the Holy Spirit in the Gospel of Luke demonstrates that the Spirit is historically and theologically of more interest to him than it was to the other evangelists. Concurrently, in the Book of Acts, Luke's second book, the key idea is ministry executed **"through the Holy Spirit."** The Book of Acts might well be re-titled, "The Continuing Acts of Jesus in the Person of the Holy Spirit through the Lives of the Apostles." Reading the Book of Acts, it becomes apparent that active discipleship and discipling is the order of the day. The person and ministry of the Holy Spirit will become more evident and meaningful to the church and the world as we become obedient to this truth as His disciples of the Spirit. Jesus told His disciples, *"I will ask the Father, and he will give you another Counselor to be with you forever—the Spirit of truth. The world cannot accept him, because it neither sees him nor knows him. But you know him, for he lives with you and will be in you" (John **14:16**, 17).*

Something new was going to happen! He who had been **with** his disciples was going to be ***in*** them. The triune God the Father, Son, and Holy Spirit would inhabit the bodies of those who believe in Jesus. He (the Holy Spirit) would continue the work Jesus began. Their discipleship was going to take on new dimensions. During the time between Christ's resurrection and His ascension, He continued to teach them in the power of the Holy Spirit (Acts 1:2). Jesus instructed them for the days immediately following His ascension, ***"Do not leave Jerusalem, but wait for the gift My Father promised, which you have heard me speak about. For John baptized with water, but in a few days you will be baptized with the Holy Spirit" (Acts 1:4, 5; Luke 24:49)***.

The fulfillment of this promise began on the day of Pentecost. But what was the meaning of Pentecost? Pentecost marked the transition from the old covenant to the new covenant and introduced the new era—the dawning of the "last days." Jesus' disciples were thrust into worldwide ministry, declaring, "\Now is the day of salvation!" They experienced being instructed as disciples of the Holy Spirit—that is, as representatives of the ascended Christ.

When the day of Pentecost arrived and the 120 believers experienced being filled with the Holy Spirit (Acts 2:1–4), ***a large crowd gathered in bewilderment and asked, "What does this mean?"*** The apostle Peter stood up and informed them that they were witnessing the fulfillment of the prophecy of the prophet Joel ***(Joel 2:28, 29): "I will pour out my Spirit on all people. Your sons and daughters will prophesy, your old men will dream dreams, your young men will see visions. Even on my servants, both men and women, I will pour out my Spirit in those days."***

After further preaching to them of Jesus Christ and His resurrection and ascension, Peter pointed to the fact what they were witnessing Christ fulfilling His promise to send the Holy Spirit. When the crowd heard this, they wanted to know what they should do in the light of the incident. Peter replied, ***"Repent and be baptized, every one of you, in the name of Jesus Christ for the forgiveness of your sins. And you will receive the gift of the Holy Spirit."*** Notice that ***"the gift"*** is actually the Holy Spirit Himself! He is the gift to the Church, and He has gifts to distribute to the church. For those who believe that this was only valid for the early church, Peter continues, ***"The promise is for you and your children and for all who are far off for all whom the Lord our God will call" (Acts 2:38, 39)***.

Jesus is our model for all things. Whatever we desire to do for God to bring the greatest glory to Him must be patterned by the Word of God and the example of Jesus Christ. The work of the Holy Spirit in us is to guide us into all truth, that Jesus might be glorified. It may surprise you to realize that Jesus Christ in His incarnation modeled for us Holy Spirit discipleship (Acts 10:38).

Chapter Three

JESUS, THE UNIQUE MODEL OF HOLY SPIRIT DISCIPLESHIP

One of the characteristics concerning Jesus Christ is that He is unique in that He is presented in Scripture as the God-Man. The greatest expression of this is found in the first eighteen verses of John's gospel (technically known as the Prologue). It is here that the apostle John gives us wonderful insight into the person of Jesus Christ and His uniqueness, which is the purpose of his writing (John 20:30, 31). The Prologue (**John 1:1–18**) unfolds a progressive revelation of Jesus Christ by means of which the average Christian may gain an understanding of his person and significance. John is the only writer who begins his story of Jesus Christ with His eternal existence rather than the time He appeared on earth. His existence at the beginning is described as the **"Word"** *(logos* in the Greek) being that **"was God"**—or, more literally, "God was the Word" (**John 1:1, 2**). The use of the term *logos* is very significant, because it was understood by both the Hebrew and Greek culture of that day.

The Jews of this time were basically Hellenistic (Greek-speaking) Jews—that is, they were Jews by nationality, but Greek culturally. By his introduction to his Gospel, John apparently seeks to establish rapport with both the Jewish and Greek readers. The term *logos* is a term that bridges the gap between these two worlds. The Jews, though Greek-speaking, would understand the term as used in the synagogue and its Old Testament equivalent Hebrew term, *davar* **(to speak)**. It denotes that

God is a speaking, revealing, and communicating God. God is said to have created the world by speaking. God said, **"'Let there be light'; and there was light" (Genesis 1:3)**, and each stage of creation was initiated by a similar **"let it be done."**

The psalmist summarizes in **Psalm 33:6: *"By the word of the Lord the heavens were made, and all the hosts by the breath of his mouth."*** John continues, ***"The Word became flesh and made his dwelling among us" (John 1:14).*** Here we have a contrast between the *being* of the eternal *logos* and the *becoming* in time of the man Christ Jesus. Marvin R. Vincent, in **Word Studies in the New Testament**, states: *"In becoming, He did not cease to be the eternal Word. His divine nature was not laid aside retaining all the essential properties of the Word. He entered into a new mode of being, not a new being" (31).*

The term *flesh* (*sarx* **in the Greek**) means more than the physical body, which would be rendered *soma*. It means human nature, including man's body, mind, soul, and moral nature. This change is not an alteration, but an addition. This is John's way of describing the incarnation; a more detailed description is found both in Matthew and Luke. The point is that now God speaks and acts through His Son, who will model for us how we can know and speak and act for the Father through the Holy Spirit. ***"In the past God spoke to our forefathers through the prophets at many times and in various ways, but in these last days he has spoken through his Son, whom he appointed heir of all things, and through whom he made the universe" (Hebrews 1:1–3).***

The Purpose of Jesus Calling Disciples

The Scriptures bear sufficient evidence that Christ modeled the work of the Father and the Holy Spirit. This modeling demonstrated what He expected of His disciples (believers) as they determined to follow Him. The Son's imitation of the Father leads to the disciples' imitation of the Son. Jesus' invitation "Come unto Me" was succeeded by the imperative "Follow Me!" which appears many times within the Gospels. Because following Christ becomes synonymous with discipleship, this phrase gains distinctive meanings from the teachings and example of Jesus. From among the many followers, Jesus chose twelve to live with Him and to represent Him **(Mark**

3:7–15). His invitation, *"Take my yoke upon you,"* becomes the next progressive step, followed by very important phrase, *"for I am meek and lowly in heart" (Matthew 11:29).*

The yoke implies a task, for discipleship is both learning and doing God's will. The Jews used the phrase "the yoke" for the idea of submission. Jesus said, *"My yoke is easy."* The word *easy* is in Greek ***chrestos***, which can mean ***well-fitting***. The ox yokes were made of wood, and each was made to custom fit the ox comfortably. Jesus is saying, "Your discipleship that you live will not be an unbearable burden. Your task will be made to fit you well and your abilities exactly."

Jesus desired to have near Him those whom He called to follow Him so that they might hear His preaching and learn of His doctrine and life. The upper room experience, as recorded in John 13, was a traumatic time for the disciples, but also a learning time as Jesus silently washed the disciples' feet, broke bread, and poured wine. Jesus followed these acts with the command to imitate His example: *"You call me 'Teacher' and 'Lord' and rightly so, for that is what I am. Now that I, your Lord and teacher, have washed your feet, you also should wash one another's Feet. I have set you an example you should do as I have done for you. I tell you the truth, no servant is greater than His master, nor is a messenger greater than the one who sent him (John 13:13–16)."*

The three years of public ministry were sufficient for Jesus to train His disciples in doctrine and demonstrate for them the manner of life they were to follow. E. J. Tinsley states: *"If his life was an imitation of the Father, their lives as disciples was to imitate him. Thereby in fact they would realize sonship loving their enemies as he did and praying for their persecutors, they would behave as sons of their father in heaven" (100).* Michael Griffiths also remarks, *"The imitation of Jesus is not, however, only a sub-conscious assimilation, but a deliberate and purposeful copying of his lifestyle" (44).*

Jesus' injunction to His disciples to be imitators of His example was later realized in the life of the apostle Paul. When writing to the Corinthian church, Paul said, ***Be imitators of me, just as I also am of Christ" (I Corinthians 11:1).*** This unapologetic statement is made, because Paul had made Jesus Christ his standard—both in word and deed. To the Thessalonians, Paul wrote, *"You became imitators [minetai] of* us and the Lord; in spite of severe suffering, you welcomed the message with joy given by the Holy Spirit. And you became a model [tupon] to all believers in Macedonia and Achaia" (I Thessalonians 1:6, 7). "For you, brothers, became imitators [minetai] of God's churches in Judea" (I Thessalonians 2:14).To the Ephesians, he wrote, *"Be kind and compassionate to one another, forgiving each other, just as in Christ God forgave you. Be imitators [minetai] of God therefore, as dearly beloved children, and live a life of love, just as Christ loved us and gave Himself up for us" (Ephesians 4:32–5:2).*

There are several things to be noted from these passages. (1) The original imitation is the imitation of God; (2) the archetypal model is the Lord Jesus Himself; (3) Paul models himself on Jesus; (4) the missionary, in turn, becomes a model to others.

The Incarnation, the Model of Perfect Discipleship

Some of the outstanding features of Jesus' incarnation that modeled discipleship were as follows. First, His relationship was with an unswerving obedience to the Father. **Jesus said,** *"My food is to do the will of Him who sent me, and to accomplish His work (John 4:34), again Jesus said, For I have come down from heaven, not to do my own will, but the will of Him who sent me" (John 6:38).*

One of Jesus' greatest desires was that in knowing Him, his disciples would also know the Father (John 17). The way to know the Father is to know Jesus, for the Father and Jesus are one. He said, "Believe me that I am in the Father, and the Father in me" (John 14:11). Later He also said, "As the Father sent me, I am sending you" (John 20:21). This implies that Jesus expects His disciples to be obedient to the Father through Him. I remember coming to the realization in my Christian walk that my obedience to Christ's teaching originated in the Father, communicated through the Son, and was affirmed and experienced in the Holy Spirit. This is what I believe Paul was expressing in Colossians 1:19, "For God [The Father] was pleased to have all his fullness dwell in him [Jesus]"and again in Colossians 2:9, 10, "For in Christ all the fullness of the Deity lives in bodily form, and you have been given fullness in Christ, who is the head over every power and authority." I trust you are beginning to see the importance of viewing Christ as the model for our discipleship. First we must understand His actions as the Son of Man, that we might more readily understand our actions as disciples of the Spirit.

Secondly, Jesus further demonstrated perfect discipleship in His submission to the work of the Holy Spirit in His life. The Holy Spirit lived in Him. Rene' Pache, commenting on ***John 2:19, said, "In speaking of His body, Jesus said, 'Destroy this temple, and in three days I will raise it up' (John 2:19)***. He certainly meant that He was the temple of the Holy Spirit, as the believer also by faith becomes His temple, though to a far lesser degree (**I Corinthians 6:19**)" (5). According to **Acts 10:38**, Jesus was anointed with the Holy Spirit and with power, and He gave testimony that this was His source of power for ministry. For example, in **Matthew 12:28**, Jesus told the Pharisees that it was by the Spirit of God that He cast out devils. The empowerment behind all of Christ's activities was not attributed to His deity, but to the anointing of the Holy Spirit. According to the synoptic gospels (Matthew, Mark, and Luke), Jesus was led by the Holy Spirit. In the context of these accounts, He was led into the wilderness to be tempted (tested) of the devil (**Matthew 4:1, 2; Mark 1:12; Luke 4:1, 2**). However, this guidance of the Holy Spirit was evidently constant in His life. We can safely say that Jesus was unceasingly taught by the Holy Spirit and guided into all truth as the Son of Man.

Luke 4:14–18 records that *"Jesus returned to Galilee in power of the Spirit and news spread throughout the whole countryside. He taught in their synagogues, and everyone praised him. He went to Nazareth, where he was brought up, and on the Sabbath day he went into the synagogue and he stood up to read. The scroll of Isaiah was handed to him. Unrolling it, he found the place where it was written: 'The Spirit of the Lord is on me, because he has anointed me to peach the good news to the poor' Jesus went on to state 'Today this scripture is fulfilled in your hearing.'"* He was affirming the Old Testament's announcement that the Messiah would be clothed with the Holy Spirit.

Lastly, it was by the fruit of the Spirit, as related in **Galatians 5:22, 23**, that Jesus modeled what God was like in character. All the virtues mentioned in Galatians 5:22, 23 were perfectly possessed by Jesus Christ. Additionally, Jesus' life of prayer, His servanthood, His self-sacrificing attitude, and His obedience to death demonstrated the depth of His discipleship. Thus, the evidence given is sufficient to challenge us, as disciples of the Holy Spirit, to follow His example.

A perceptive article by Larry W. Hurtado, Professor of New Testament Language, Literature, and Theology, in ***Patterns of Discipleship in the New Testament***, states: ***"In Mark's account, Jesus is both the basis for and the pattern of discipleship and the servant pattern that they are to follow (Mark 10:43–45). In fact, Mark makes Jesus the only adequate model of discipleship" (25).*** Hurtado continues, ***"If we recognize that Mark intended to present Jesus as the true model of Christian discipleship and that Mark's narrative was shaped to make the story of Jesus the blueprint for the lives and ministry of all his disciples, then we have probably only grasped what was staring us in the face all along in the caption to the Gospel in Mark 1:1, 'The beginning (arche) of the gospel of Jesus Christ' is probably to be taken as referring to Mark's entire account of Jesus. That is, the*** 'beginning' of the message and mission to which all future disciples are summoned" (27).

It certainly makes sense that Jesus' life would be the pattern or model for His disciples, since they would be endowed by the Holy Spirit, who would build Christ's character in them. They would not simply proclaim His truths, but they would demonstrate His life to others. This is what separates the discipleship of Christianity from other forms of discipleship that pertained to the teachings of the philosophers, as well as the Jewish rabbis' disciples of New Testament times. Disciples of the Spirit display the fruits of the Spirit, which reflect the quality life of Jesus—love, joy, peace, patience, kindness, goodness, faithfulness, gentleness, and self-control. We are living in the dispensation of the Holy Spirit, in which we should be demonstrating these virtues in our troubled world today.

Understand that if we make disciples who make disciples, our churches will succeed. Follow the model Jesus used when he made disciples: be an intentional leader and disciple in a relational environment, seeing others as potential disciplers to their individual worlds of influence. Jesus imparted ***character*** by ***example*** and ***modeling***. He modeled both a strategy and lifestyle. The Scriptures are clear that the Holy Spirit operated through Jesus, demonstrating His power and ministry to others. In **Luke 3:22**, "The Holy Spirit descended upon Him like a dove"; in **Luke 4:1**, "Jesus, full of the Holy Spirit was led by the Holy Spirit." **Matthew 12:28** says,

"But if I drive out demons by the Spirit of God, then the kingdom of God has come upon you." There are many other references that give evidence of the Holy Spirit in Jesus, and **Acts 10:38 summarizes by stating,** *"God anointed Jesus of Nazareth with the Holy Spirit and Power, and how he went around doing good and healing all who were under the power of the devil, because God was with him."* Why should it be difficult for us to believe that we can have the Holy Spirit, and as disciples of the Holy Spirit, do wonderful works in His name? We are disciples following Jesus' model.

Chapter Four

THE ETHICAL FOUNDATION FOR DISCIPLES OF THE HOLY SPIRIT

The Ethics of Jesus as Seen in the Sermon on the Mount

It is important, as disciples of the Holy Spirit, to recognize that we are governed by specific ethical principles. Christian ethics is almost entirely based upon the Scriptures. Henlee Barnette, a leading Baptist minister, defines Christian ethics as *"a systematic explanation of the moral example and teaching of Jesus applied to the total life of the individual in society and actualized by the power of the Spirit."* It is in the Sermon on the Mount that we discover the ethics of Jesus. However, it is not a list of moral precepts that provides good advice on how to live, nor is it a picture of life in some far-off kingdom age that has no relevance for the church. On the contrary, I believe that the Sermon on the Mount is relevant to the Church in our present day. There is no teaching to be found in the Sermon which is not also found in the various Epistles. Make a list of the teachings; then read the Epistles.

All the Epistles are meant for Christians today; so if their teachings are the same as the Sermon on the Mount, clearly its teaching also is meant for us today. The Sermon on the Mount is a picture of what the inner character of the follower of Jesus in any age should be like. It describes what human life and human community look like when they come under the gracious rule of God. The sermon is not a program one must follow in order to become a disciple but is the way of life that is pursued by those who are disciples. This becomes vitally important when we are involved with the spiritual gifts of the church and their operations, which will be discussed in later chapters. As Jesus revealed these truths to his disciples, his desire was that, by the appropriation of these teachings, his followers would, in time, under the discipleship of the Holy Spirit, reveal both what God was like in character and the nature of his kingdom. His followers were to let their lights shine from their lives so that all would see their good deeds and bring praise to the Father in heaven (**Matthew 5:16**). Someone said that these should be seen as simply "attitudes how to be." That's a good way of thinking about these truths.

The beatitudes speak to the inner righteousness one must possess to be part of the kingdom. It is important to recognize that these qualities expressed by Christ were also possessed by Him. John Stott expresses this fact so well in *The Message of the Sermon on the Mount* as he states: *"We see him as he is in himself, in his heart, motives, and in the secret place with his Father. We also see him in the arena of public life, in his relations with his fellow men, showing mercy, making peace, being persecuted, acting like salt, letting his light shine, loving and serving others (even his enemies), and devoting himself above all to the extension of God's kingdom and righteousness in the world" (24).*

It is not my intent to expound the whole sermon, but to glean the required ethos (character) that a disciple of the Holy Spirit should possess, as seen in the opening Beatitudes.

The Beatitudes: Righteousness in its Essential Inner Characteristics (Matthew 5:3–12)

The beatitudes point to eight distinguishable features of Christian character and conduct, especially in relation to God and to men. Divine blessing is promised to those who reveal these features.

Blessed are the poor in spirit, for theirs is the kingdom of heaven.

This is key to all that follows. It means a complete absence of pride, self-assurance, and self reliance. It means a consciousness that we are nothing in the presence of God. It is that characteristic which makes a man see himself as he really is. As the result, he is humble and willing to seek help. It is the opposite of self-righteousness, self-sufficiency, and self-glorification. As a prerequisite to becoming disciples of the Holy Spirit, we must depend on God to bring us into a new status of receiving the riches of His grace, replacing our poverty in spirit.

Blessed are those who mourn, for they will be comforted.

To mourn is something that follows of necessity from being "poor in spirit." As I confront God and His holiness and contemplate the life that I am meant to live, I see myself, my utter helplessness, and my hopelessness. D. Martyn Lloyd Jones, in **Studies in the Sermon of the Mount,** says, *"The man who truly mourns because of his sinful state and condition is a man who is going to repent; he is, indeed, actually repenting already. And the man who truly repents as the result of the work of the Holy Spirit upon him, is a man who is certain to be led to the Lord Jesus Christ" (60)*. Notice that we are witnessing the process of obtaining righteousness necessary to reveal the character of Christ in us as his disciples indwelt by the Holy Spirit.

Blessed are the meek, for they will inherit the earth.

Meekness signifies a state of mind which has no thoughts of self-assertion. It is the antithesis of pride and self-seeking. Jesus certainly modeled meekness in His life, but it was by no means a display of weakness or timidity. In fact, true meekness reveals the strength of one's character. It is a compassionate use of one's strength for the good of others. Consider how the apostle Paul so aptly spoke of this about Jesus in **Philippians 2:4–7** as he pointed to the attitude of Jesus as an example of how we should think and act. "Let this mind be in you, which was also in Christ Jesus," in that Jesus willingly laid aside his rights as the divine Son of God to give Himself as a servant for humanity. The word *meek* comes from a Hebrew root meaning *"to be bowed down."* The Greek word ***praus*** is associated with humility, lowliness, gentleness, peacefulness, mildness, patience, and adaptability.

Blessed are those who hunger and thirst for righteousness.

To hunger and thirst really means to be desperate, to be starving, to feel life is ebbing out, and to realize an urgent need for help. Have you ever hungered and been thirsty? Most of us in our western culture have difficulty comprehending what this really means. I recall hearing of a missionary who was returning home for a time of furlough retelling an experience he had while waiting for a connecting flight home. As he entered the airport terminal, to his surprise, he saw a fellow missionary, who was also returning home. After fond greetings and surprised laughter, they decided to get something to eat at the nearby restaurant. While they were sharing their experiences, their meal was served. After they offered thanks to the Lord, they began to eat the meal, and they both were very displeased with the meal, and with disgust, pushed it aside and returned to their conversation. They proceeded to pay the check and move toward the terminal to resume their flights. As they were leaving, they noticed three boys who had been standing in the doorway of the restaurant. The boys suddenly rushed to the abandoned table and quickly stuffed their pockets and mouths with the rejected food and then fled the restaurant. The missionary said, "For the first time in my life, I realized that I did not know what it meant to be hungry!" Those boys did not evaluate or examine the food—it didn't matter; they were hungry and desperate. Hungering and thirsting is the opposite of nominal Christian living; it is the opposite of spiritual apathy and moral indifference; it is the opposite of ho-hum Christianity. It is marked by a strong desire to do what is right and have the ability to do so, not content to just get by. Hungering and thirsting after righteousness issues a strong desire to be free from sin and all its manifestations. It is a panting after godliness, Christ-likeness, purity, goodness, truthfulness, and holiness of heart. David expressed in ***Psalm 42, "As the deer pants for streams of water, so my soul pants for you, O God. My soul thirsts for God, for the living God."***

This is one blessing that God desires to give, because He imputes His righteousness to us, which is life's ultimate gift. Remember, God is going to create a new heaven and new earth, where righteousness will dwell for eternity. What a blessed day that will be for the children of God! Up until this point, we have been looking at disciples in terms of their needs and the consciousness of their needs. But now the turning point is the disposition of the disciple, which results from what has gone on before.

Blessed are the merciful.

This signifies the quality of mind, which can think itself into the minds of others. The word ***merciful*** might well be translated as the ability to feel human emotions, to identify with the problems of others, to be able to humanize one's feelings and manifest them in action, to be gracious, to console, or to bring help to others. It is closely related to the word ***compassion***. It is interesting to note that the motivational gifts mentioned in Roman 12 include the gift of mercy. Mercy shows itself best in the ability to be afflicted with the same feelings as another. A merciful person is one who has become "other-centered." This is important in understanding how we approach the work of God, considering ourselves as part of the body of Christ. Remember that the Scriptures portray God as a merciful God (Deuteronomy 4:31; Nehemiah 9:31; Psalm 25:6; Ephesians 2:4).

Blessed are the pure in heart.

According to the general usage of the term, the heart refers to the center of personality. In some cases, it means the seat of affection and emotions. It is the fount out of which everything flows. It includes the mind, the will, and the emotions. It is the total man, and that is what our Lord emphasized. Purity in heart is not merely on the surface, but in the center of one's being. This is illustrated in the story of the prodigal son **(Luke 15)**. The son had come to the end of his riotous living, and **Luke 15:17** says, *"when he came to his senses,"* he reacted in his total being. In his mind, he said, *"**How many of my father's hired men have food to spare, and here I am starving to death!**"* Then his emotions kicked in, and he said, *"**I will say to my father, 'I have sinned against heaven and against you. I am no longer worthy to be called your son; make me like one of your hired men.'**"* Then his will was activated, and he proceeded on his journey home to his father. The word *pure* carries a double meaning: (1)

Purity, in a religious sense, is a person who is morally clean, spiritual holy, and ethically righteous. It is the opposite of being dirty-minded, ungodly, and sinful. (2) Purity, in the emotional and psychological sense, wears no masks; it does nothing sneaky, it has no secrets. It loves to walk in the light, under the scrutiny of God **(I John 1:5–9)**. What does it mean "they will see God"? I used to think this was referring to heaven, when we will see God face-to-face. But as I viewed these beatitudes, I realized they are applicable to our lives here and now, even though it is true that the pure in heart will see God fully in the future. However, a disciple of the Holy Spirit is able to discern God in every avenue of his life. Perception of life is above the natural, with an understanding of God and an awareness of His presence. It means to have insight into the ways of God and the inner assurance of His existence.

Blessed are the peacemakers.

The Greek word *eirene* means "unity, harmony, quiet." It is the opposite of a quarrelsome, faultfinding, critical spirit. **Hebrews 12:14 says, *"Make every effort to live in peace with all men and to be holy; without holiness no one will see the Lord."*** This beatitude calls for an active involvement in bringing about reconciliation between those in conflict, whether in public or at a personal level. This attitude is importance in church situations. As a pastor, I regretted having to deal with conflict in church situations, whether with the congregation collectively or with individuals.

I remember one particular situation where there was much conflict over a proposal that had been made at our denominational convention. A group of pastors had proposed to change our denominational name. There was heated debate which almost escalated to the point of physical violence. The meeting was out of control, and every effort to restore order had failed until the president, who was highly respected, stepped down from the platform, knelt at the altar rail, and wept. Suddenly, there was a holy hush, and ministers and delegates began to move toward the altar. The auditorium was filled with cries of repentance, which resulted in praise and embracing one another. I never forgot that moment when seeing how one man's attitude of humility changed that emotionally charged group from a screaming mob to a praising, reconciling, forgiving, loving group of saints.

I recall another situation when several thousand gathered in Washington, D.C. for a protest march and rally that broke out in violence. The news media focused their cameras on a number of violent incidents. A number of students from the college where I taught attended this gathering to be witnesses for Christ and promote peace where they could. This group brought back many photos of incidents where Christians were ministering to those who were hurt physically as a result of the violence. Among some of the pictures, they showed a number of Mennonites (who are considered pacifists) giving medical aid and praying with those who were afflicted. Of course, the news media never focused on these peacemakers—but God did! Peace is not gained without effort; peacemaking is exceedingly difficult at times. One must become positive and go out of his or her way to look for means and methods of making peace. True peacemaking involves seeking heart-to-heart reconciliation between people. We tend to think of the Holy Spirit only in the sense of power and might. One of the great symbols of the Spirit is the dove demonstrating peace and gentleness. As we recognize that we are disciples of the Holy Spirit, we should experience a balance between the power of the Spirit and the peace of the Spirit in our life and activities. In effect, this beatitude means, "blessed are those who make this world a better place for all men to live."

Abraham Lincoln once said: **"Die when I may, I would like it to be said of me, that I always pulled up a weed and planted a flower where I thought a flower would grow."** As we reflected on these beatitudes, we recognized that Jesus expressed the importance of what His disciples were inside more than how they appeared outwardly. What we are outwardly reflects what we are within. As we identify ourselves today as disciples indwelt by the Holy Spirit, the beatitudes should be much more evident in our lives and recognized by others.

The Ethics of Jesus Manifested in the Apostle Paul and Other Apostles

The apostle Paul, who was probably the greatest disciple of Jesus Christ in the ancient world, urges these same ethical teachings for the disciples of the Holy Spirit dispensation. The conversion of Saul (Paul) proved the power of Christianity to overcome the strongest prejudices and give outstanding testimony to the work of the Holy Spirit in changing a man's life and direction **(Acts 9:1–31)**. Paul, in his zealous adherence to Judaism, was determined to exterminate Christianity. With increased zeal to destroy this movement, he obtained letters from the high priest to the synagogues in Damascus to search out those who claimed to be disciples this "way." As he proceeded on his journey, he suddenly experienced a flash of light around him, and he fell to the ground. This pompous, proud Pharisee found himself groveling in the dust, trembling, and no doubt perplexed, as he heard a voice, "Saul, Saul, why are you harassing and persecuting Me?"

When Saul inquired, *"Who are you, Lord?"* the answer came: *"I am Jesus, whom you are persecuting."* Jesus told Saul to get up and go into the city, and he would be told what to do. Saul, getting up from the ground, discovered he was blind and had to be led to Damascus by those who accompanied him. Imagine this man who was so radical and fearless becoming broken and contrite, entering Damascus to be instructed by a disciple named Ananias of the movement he was trying to destroy. Ananias proceeded to lay hands on Saul, and his sight was restored. Ananias then instructed Saul in the faith and baptized him, and he was filled with the Holy Spirit. From then on, Saul gave his life to following Jesus and making Him known. As sign of his conversion, he changed his name from Saul to Paul (meaning (**"little"**). Paul demonstrated what it meant to have a radical commitment to Christ as a disciple of the Holy Spirit and as an apostle. Now, instead of pursuing the Christians and terrorizing them, Paul found himself joined to the people of God. He was brought to life by the Spirit to live his life in Christ and for Christ. Paul's greatest confession is found when he was imprisoned. He seeks to encourage the Philippian believers that what was happening to him was serving to advance the gospel. Paul wrote: *"I eagerly expect and hope that I in no way will be ashamed, but will have sufficient courage so that now as always Christ will be exalted in my body, whether by life or by death For me to live is Christ and to die is gain. If I am to go on living in the body, this will mean fruitful labor for me" (Philippians 1:20–22)*.

We are saved and brought to life by the Spirit so we can live the Christlike life, and by walking in the Spirit and being led by the Spirit, the Spirit's fruit in our lives begins to build the character of Christ in us. That's what Christian ethics is all about. **Gordon Fee states:** *"Christian ethics is not primarily and individualistic one-on-one with God brand of personal holiness; Rather it has to do with living the life of the Spirit in Christian community and the world" (Paul, the Spirit and the People of God, 99).* Paul was always concerned about the community of faith and the local church. He was greatly concerned with the ethics of Christ being displayed in the community of believers, since they represented the body of Christ **(Ephesians 5:15–21)**. The point that needs to be made here is that Christian ethics were vital to all the apostles, as they had to deal with the various churches. The apostle Paul, in his dealing with the conduct of the Corinthian church concerning the operation of the gifts of the Spirit, found that the lack of ethical principles was at the heart of their problem.

The apostle Peter attempted to encourage those who were scattered and persecuted throughout Asia minor and help them to deal ethically with their situation. The apostle James also added practical, down-to-earth principles. He challenged his readers to the proper "behavior of belief"that is, his letter consisted of a series of tests to their faith. What they professed to believe, he insisted, must be evident by how they live. In turn, the apostle John, in his epistles, directed his concern about a heresy which had sprung up in the early church. It was called the "Gnostic Heresy," which was threatening the fellowship of believers (similar to the New Age doctrine today). He defended the deity and incarnation of Christ and their true fellowship in Him. One great testimony of Scripture is that its doctrinal unity and ethical principles, expressed by the apostles Paul, Peter, James, and John, all support and adhere to the ethic of Jesus Christ. I have been especially impressed to find how much Paul expresses the ethics of the Sermon on the Mount throughout his epistles. Let's look at a few examples:

"Blessed are the poor in spirit: for theirs is the kingdom of heaven" (Matthew 5:3). *"Christ Jesus humbled Himself (by) becoming obedient to death even death on a cross!"* **(Philippians 2:8)** *"Even though I was once a blasphemer, and a persecutor, and a violent man, I was shown mercy. Christ Jesus came into the world to save sinners—of whom I am worst" (I Timothy 1:13–15).*

"Blessed are those who mourn, for they will be comforted" (Matthew 5:4). *"For just as the sufferings of Christ flow over into our lives, so also through Christ our comfort overflows" (II Corinthians 1:5).* "And you are proud (puffed up)! Shouldn't you rather have been filled with grief" (I Corinthians 1:2). "For you became sorrowful as God intended Godly sorrow brings repentance that leads to salvation" (II Corinthians 7:9, 10).

"Blessed are the meek, for they will inherit the earth" (Matthew 5:5). *"By meekness and gentleness of Christ, I appeal to you" (II Corinthians 10:1). "To be peaceable and considerate, and to show true humility (meekness) toward all men" (Titus 3:2).*

"Blessed are those who hunger and thirst for righteousness for they will be filled" (Matthew 5:6). *"For the grace of God that brings salvation has appeared it teaches us to say 'No' to ungodliness and worldly passions and live self-controlled lives in this present age" (Titus 2:11, 12).* "For in the gospel a righteousness from God is revealed, a righteousness that is by faith from first to last, just as it is written 'The righteous will live by faith'" (Romans 1:17). "Flee the evil desires of youth, and pursue righteousness, faith, love and peace, along with those who call on the Lord out of a pure heart" (II Timothy 2:22).

"Blessed are the merciful, for they will be shown mercy" (Matthew 5:7). *"But for his great love for us, God, who is rich in mercy made us alive with Christ* (Ephesians 2:4). "May the Lord show mercy to the household of Onesiphorus, because he often refreshed me and was not ashamed of my chains" May the Lord grant that he will find mercy from the Lord on that day!" (II Timothy 1:16, 18).

"Blessed are the pure in heart: for they will see God" (Matthew 5:8). *"The goal of this command is love, which comes from a pure heart and a good conscience and a sincere faith" (I Timothy 1:5). "Finally, brothers, whatever is true, whatever is noble, whatever is right, whatever is pure, whatever is lovely, what ever is admirable— if anything is excellent or praise worthy, think about such things" (Philippians 4:8).*

"Blessed are the peacemakers: for they shall be called the sons of God" (Matthew 5:9). *"The kingdom of God is. peace. in the Holy Spirit. Let us therefore make every effort to do what leads to peace and to mutual edification" (Romans 14:17, 19). "Let the peace of Christ rule in your hearts, since as members of one body you were called to peace" (Colossians 3:15).*

Though we have primarily focused on Paul, these same ethical values are found in other apostles Peter, James, and John. Though their writings are not as voluminous as Paul's, nevertheless, there are no contradictions between these apostles, since they all focused upon the ethical teachings of Christ. Consider a few examples from each of them in their understanding and agreement with Paul. I choose not to give as much detail here, since I think my observation has been made clear in terms of the importance of the ethical foundation needed to maintain and govern the church and bring glory to God.

The Apostle Peter

Peter refers to mercy (**I Peter 1:3; 2:10**), humility (**1 Peter 5:5, 6**), suffering (**I Peter 2:19–23**), and righteousness (**I Peter 2:24, 3:11; II Peter 2:21, 3:14**). Peter expresses many virtues that should be found in believers (**II Peter 1:3–8**).

The Apostle James

It has been said that if John rested on Jesus' bosom, James sat at his feet. James preserves more of Christ's teaching than the writers of all the other epistles combined. He never actually quotes his older brother, but he seems to constantly refer to his teachings as the basis of his own. There are a number of parallels to Jesus' Sermon on the Mount. Read James, and you will eventually recall some statement made by Jesus.

Epistle of James	Matthew's Sermon on the Mount
1:2	5:10–12
1:4	5:48
1:5, 17	7:7–12
1:9	5:13
1:20	5:22
2:13	6:14, 15

2:14	7:21–23
3: 17, 18	5:9
4:4	6:24
4:10	5:3, 4

In studying ethical concerns of the biblical writers, I became more and more convinced that we need to recognize that we are to be disciples of the Holy Spirit. I realize that this may seem like a radical concept to some people. However, I have attempted to deal with this earlier in the book concerning the directive of Christ for His disciples to be empowered and guided by the Holy Spirit in their lives and ministry, since He ascended to the Father's right hand **(Acts 2:33)**.

It is imperative that, as we approach the end of the age, the church take a greater concern for understanding the ministry of the Holy Spirit. The fruit of the Holy Spirit and the gifts of the Holy, Spirit properly understood, are the only hope for the Church to be effective in these last days. There must be a greater sensitivity to the person of the Holy Spirit and His power encompassed in holiness, humility, and compassion. Too often, we portray Him as a highly emotional being, displaying the unusual and the spectacular. The Holy Spirit undergirds the whole range of Christian experience, from beginning to end. I heard someone describe the Holy Spirit as "God's vending machine" that distributes whatever we want, whenever we want it. He is not under our control; we are under His control. As we approach chapter five of the book, which deals with the fruit of the Spirit and the gifts of the Spirit, consider the following guidelines:

1. The Holy Spirit was given so the Church might truly be the body of Christ, sharing His life, faithfully manifesting His character, and being fruitful in every good work (Romans 8:29; Galatians 5:16–26). This is the basic evidence of the Spirit's presence and work. To stress the gifts of the Spirit at the expense of the ethical is not only to distort the gospel, but also to invite judgment upon ourselves (Acts 8:18–24).
2. The Holy Spirit was given to the church to empower it for the task of bearing witness to Christ (Acts 1:8). A powerful evangelistic ministry in word and deed which is effective

in making disciples among all nations is one of the most immediate and primary results of the Spirit's work since Pentecost.

3. In brief, it is the work of the Spirit to interpret and vitalize the gospel in the lives of God's people in all His manifold and rich dimensions, that the church, in turn, may become part of the good news of God's grace and purpose, commending its truth to the world. The challenge that Christians face, both individually and collectively, is how to live in the Christian community and the world. Gordon Fee states this very well in his book, **Paul, the Spirit, and the People of God,** "Two issues confront us. First, that Christian ethics is not primarily an individualistic one-on-one- with- God brand of personal holiness; rather it has to do with living the life of the Spirit in Christian community (p.99).

The apostles (especially Paul) never left ethics as unrealistic, idealistic goals on paper. Paul was no Don Quixote, chasing windmills of impossible dreams. He moved from principle to practice in his letters to the churches. He told them what Spirit's ethics (or fleshed-out behavior) looks like and where the power source to live comes from. It is important that we recognize what we experience on the individual level, and we must keep in mind how it applies to the community of believers to whom we belong. I remember attending a revival meeting being held in a local neighborhood church. I had only been a Christian for a short time and was interested in understanding the true meaning of worship in a community setting. I became very confused throughout the service. There seemed to be no particular order and direction, as one person would express themselves in tongues, another in dancing and running up and down the aisle, another in giving some kind of prophecy, and so on. At that moment, I was perplexed and apprehensive of what was going on. There was a lack of control and no explanation for me to gain some understanding. Months later, after receiving further understanding, I found these were legitimate expressions of worship, but they lacked ethical sensitivity to the total community and those who may have been visiting. When we observe the forming of the early church following Pentecost, we see that there were a number of churches in need of instruction and direction. There were two churches I would like to mention to which Paul gave definite instructions namely, the church in Galatia and the church in Corinth. Paul unwraps the ethics of Jesus in two parts: the fruit (or character of the Spirit) in a believer's life and the gifts (the work of the Spirit) in a believer's life. In some later chapters, we will discuss the importance of ethical understanding and behavior in the operation of the gifts in the church. Let us begin to look at these two aspects and their importance to disciples of the Holy Spirit.

Chapter Five

DISCIPLES OF THE HOLY SPIRIT: THE FRUIT DIMENSION

As we discussed earlier, as a result of His resurrection and then ascension into heaven, Christ wanted to make clear to His disciples that they would be disciples under the direction of the Holy Spirit. Christ would be present with them and in them by the person of the Holy Spirit (**John 14:15–17**). The Holy Spirit would indwell them and develop the fruit of Christ's character in them. The Holy Spirit would also empower them and distribute gifts for ministry. Thus, we have two dimensions of the work of the Holy Spirit namely, the fruit, or character dimension, and the gifts, or ministry dimension. I would like to consider these dimensions separately and later show the importance of their integration within the believer and their operation together in the body of Christ.

The Fruit Dimension in the Life of the Disciples (Galatians 5:16–26)

This has to do with the ethical and moral aspects that represent the character of Christ. Jesus, in speaking to His disciples of their relationship with Him, illustrated it as the vine and its branches (**John 15**). The branches (disciples) could only bear fruit as the remained connected to the vine (Christ), and His life would flow through them and reveal His character in them. The fruit of the Spirit is love, which has in it the seed for still more fruit, which we will see in a moment. As we are the body of Christ (the Church), we are to reveal what Christ is like in His character. One of the most striking and challenging admonitions of the apostle Paul is for believers to "walk in the Spirit." What does it mean to walk in the Spirit? In order to understand this, we need to see that the Galatian Christians were being influenced by legalistic Jews who insisted that Christians must continue walking in the law as well as in grace. Paul insisted that Christ had fulfilled the law and had become the end of the law to everyone who believed in Him. The reign of law had ended, and the time for the reign of grace had come. Unfortunately, this liberty was being interpreted as license to lift all restraints and do whatever one desired. Paul warned that Christian liberty must be expressed by obedience to the law of love. To walk is to pursue our daily tasks under the guidance of the Holy Spirit and meet every situation with His help. If we are truly disciples of the Holy Spirit, we will not yield to sinful desires of the flesh. Our desires become those that God desires for us and His purpose in us. How can this be accomplished? Certainly we cannot even entertain the idea that this can be accomplished in our own strength. We must continue to emphasize that we are disciples of the Holy Spirit under and through the authority of Jesus Christ. Therefore, consider the following admonitions:

The Works of the Flesh Challenged by the Holy Spirit (Galatians 5:16–21, 24)

The term *flesh* here refers to our sinful nature, and there is a definite conflict between our sinful nature and the Spirit **(Galatians 5:16, 17)**. The Christian cannot simply will to overcome the flesh. The solution is not to pit our will against the flesh, but to surrender our will to the Holy Spirit. The Holy Spirit writes God's law of love on our hearts **(Hebrews 10:14–17)**. These works can be divided into three major categories:

Carnal Sins: Relating to physical or especially sexual pleasures: sexual immorality (adultery, fornication) and debauchery (uncleanness—filthiness of heart and mind). Three Greek words are used that relate to our present day: *porneia,* where we get the terms **pornography and prostitute;** *akatharsia*, which expresses uncleanness, dirty-mindedness, and impurity; and *aselgeia*, which translates as **sensuality** or love of sin so reckless that one ceases to care what God thinks or man thinks of his actions. This certainly is a commentary of our times.

Irrational Sins: This includes idolatry, witchcraft, ***pharmakeia*** **(use of drugs)**, and superstitious sins. The use of drugs has permeated the ancient world and certainly has become a menace and destroyer of our world today. However, there is a legitimate use of drugs prescribed by medical doctors and pharmacists. The investigation of horoscopes, the power of crystals, and the New Age movement of our time are good examples of irrational sins.

Social Sins: Hatred, violence, discord, jealousy, rage, selfish ambition, dissensions, factions, envy, drunkenness, and orgies (wild parties). This is enmity between man and man. It is also man out of control of himself. Our society today raises its fist up to God and their fellowman and says, "I'll do what I please, and I don't care about you or anyone else; it's my life."

The Indwelling Spirit Develops and Produces Fruit in the Disciple (Galatians 5:22–23, 25, 26)

When we think of ***works,*** we think of effort, labor, and toil. When we think of ***fruit,*** we think of beauty, quietness, and the unfolding of life. The flesh produces dead works, but the Spirit produces living fruit that is appealing and beautiful.

The Characteristics God Desires to See in the Disciple of the Holy Spirit (Galatians 5:22, 23)

Charles Hummel, in ***Fire in the Fireplace,*** states *"that the fullness of the Spirit evidenced by a Christ-like character in the last analysis the value of all we do depends on who we are; apart from right attitudes and motives even out best actions mean nothing" (117).* The characteristics that God desires are those found in His Son, Jesus Christ.

The epistle of Hebrews describes Him in a beautiful way. *"The Son is the radiance of God's glory and the exact representation of his being"* **(Hebrews 1:3)**. Is this not God's desire to have His children reflect His dignity, majesty, and power? If we are the body of Christ and indwelt by the Holy Spirit, we are going to manifest Him. In ***Mere Christianity,*** C.

S. Lewis says the reason for the whole of Christianity and the existence of the church is to draw people to Christ and to make persons Christlike in all of life. Paul shows how this is expressed in the nine-fold fruit of the Spirit. He is listing the great qualities in the fruit of the Spirit—love, joy, peace, patience, kindness, goodness, faithfulness, gentleness, and self-control. The fruit of the Spirit is love, and all other forms are an outgrowth of love. I would like to divide the list into three groups, which I think will give a better understanding and appreciation of these wonderful truths.

Life in the Spirit expressed toward God: *Love, Joy, and Peace*

The word for love here is ***agape,*** which is the highest form of love—divine love. **Romans 5:5** says this love is God's gift to us: "**God has poured out His love into our hearts by the Holy Spirit, whom he has given to us.**" There are several words for love in the Greek language: **(1)** ***Eros,*** which means the passionate, physical love of a man for a woman. We get the word ***erotic*** from this form, which we associate with lust. Our present culture is permeated by the erotic expression of love. It is never used in the New Testament. **(2)** ***Philia*** was considered the highest form of human love. It speaks of the highest level of friendship. Friendship arises out of mere companionship—when two or more of the companions discover that they have in common some insight or interest which others do not share. In **John 21:15–17**, this term was used by Peter when Jesus posed the question, "Peter, do you love me?" Jesus used the word ***agape,*** meaning divine unconditional love. Peter answered, ***"Yes Lord, you know that I love you."*** Peter, however, used the word ***philia,*** expressing friendship. Jesus pressed the issue three times, and all three times, Peter gave the same answer. Finally, the third time Jesus asked, in effect, ***"Well, Peter, do you really philia me?*** Okay, I will accept this for now; ***go and shepherd My sheep."*** Peter never discerned what Jesus was asking, but after Pentecost, Peter devoted his life to live and express Christ's ***agape*** love. **(3)** ***Storge*** is basically family love parental love to a child and the child's love to parents. The nuclear family was not the norm in ancient times, so ***storge*** probably had a much wider reference. Presumably, it embraced uncles, aunts, grandparents, and many more relatives. Membership in a family meant a great deal to most people in antiquity. **(4) *Agape*** is the term that defines God Himself, for **I John 4:16** declares, "God is Love. Whoever lives in love lives in God, and God in Him." This love is produced in the heart of the yielded believer by the Holy Spirit. This is why the term *fruit* is used instead of *works* because the Christian experience is the product of a new and divine life implanted in the believer. It is an unconditional love; its chief ingredient is self-sacrifice for the benefit of the one loved **(John 3:16)**.

Juan Carlos Ortiz, in his book, ***Disciple***, stresses how ***agape love*** is the highest form of love by the following comparisons. He first refers to "neighbor love" **(Leviticus 19:18)**, where we are to love our neighbor as ourselves. It means I must wish for my neighbor the same thing I wish for myself. This is a minimal form of love, since it is selfishly based upon love for ourselves. Another form of love is expressed as "brother love" **(John 13:34)**—a command to love our brother as Christ loved us. This degree of love is meant for the church—the family of God. It is the type of love to rule over the Christian community. This is certainly a higher, commendable love, but Ortiz says God requires a higher level of love, which he refers to as "Trinity love," consisting of God the Father, God the Son, and God the Holy Spirit. To explain Trinity love, he gives the explanation with potatoes. Each potato plant has several potatoes under it. When they are harvested, they are dug up, placed together in a sack, and regrouped. But they are not united. When they are washed and peeled, they think they are closer, yet they must be cut in pieces and mixed. They now lose their individuality. They now think they are ready for their master. But what God wants is mashed potatoes! Not many potatoes—one mashed potato. What's the point? God the Father, and the Son, and the Holy Spirit are one in essence and love and minister that love together to us so that we display "mashed potato love" to each other. It is a love of essence, where when one member rejoices, we all rejoice; when one member suffers, we all suffer.

When disciples of the Holy Spirit live in the sphere of love, then they experience **joy**. Joy should not be mistaken as merely expressing happiness. A person walking through his neighborhood came across a man sitting on a bench in the park, stooped over, with his face in his hands, showing signs of depression and sadness. He inquired, "Sir, can I be of any help to you?"

"No, thank you, nobody can help me, I'm just tired of being unhappy!" the man answered. "Surely things can't be all that bad. Hey! I know someone who can help you. There's a carnival on the other side of this park, and they have a clown there that has the greatest ability to get people laughing and forgetting their troubles. How about coming with me to see him?" The man looked up and said, "Mister, you don't understand; I happen to be that clown you're talking about!" We can give the impression that we have joy and happiness but be dreadfully sad inside. Every human being is hungry for joy. Jesus said the joy that a Christian experiences is from entering the kingdom of God, which the apostle Paul describes in **Romans 14:17:** *"For the kingdom of God is not a matter of eating and drinking, but of righteousness, peace and joy in the Holy Spirit."* Intimate relationship with Jesus is the source of joy. The believer's joy is produced within by the Holy Spirit. The unbeliever's joy depends on outward stimulations and circumstances. The New Testament often links joy with persecution, as seen in **James 1:2:** *"Consider it pure joy, my bothers, whenever you face trials of many kinds, because you know the testing of your faith develops perseverance."* Peter, in speaking of how we are looking forward to Christ's being revealed in the last times, also reminds them in **I Peter 1:6–9** that *"In this you greatly rejoice, though now for a little while you may have to suffer grief in all kinds of trials. These have come so that you faith—of greater worth than gold, which perishes even though refined by fire—may proved genuine and may result in praise, glory and honor when Jesus Christ is revealed. Though you have not seen him, you love him; even though you do not see him now, you believed in him and are filled with an inexpressible and glorious joy, for you are receiving the goal of your faith, the salvation of you."* Someone said, **"Joy is love, smiling."** When a person lives in the sphere of love, he experiences joy. Love and joy together produce peace.

Philippians 4:4, 7: *"Rejoice in the Lord always. I will say it again: rejoice! .And the peace of God, which transcends all understanding, will guard your hearts and your minds in Christ Jesus."* The New Testament links peace directly to Jesus. God the God of peace, who alone brings peace has acted in Jesus to bring the blessings of peace to us. This peace is not the absence of difficulties or trials, but it is demonstrated in our heart in the midst of these things. I remember seeing a painting some years ago that depicted a thundering waterfall dashing on the rocks below and exploding, its water spraying upward, demonstrating great power. I was perplexed when I saw that the title of the painting was "Peace." I studied the painting more closely to try to understand why the artist would give it that title. As I looked more closely, my eyes were directed to the top corner of the picture, which displayed a tree branch hanging over the falls, which carried a nest of little birds and the mother, feeding them. I remember exclaiming, "Wow! What an example of peace!" That's the peace that God's children should experience in this world. The term "Peace" in the New Testament is the Greek word *eirene* (there are ninety occurrences of it in the New Testament) and is defined and enriched by the Old Testament term *shalom*, which conveys the idea of wholeness, unity, and harmony. Therefore, the use of the term *peace* is rooted in one's relationship with God, and in turn, the restoration of human beings to inner harmony and harmonious relationships with others. All these three qualities—love, joy, and peace—express the Godward aspect of the Christian life.

Life in the Spirit as expressed with others: *Patience, Kindness, and Goodness*

Remember, the fruit (singular) of the Spirit is *love* and is the main fruit from which all other attributes are expressions of that single fruit, *love*. It is God's love being distributed into our hearts and lives so others can see and experience Him through us. As we proceed to the second division of the fruit of the Spirit, we discover three attributes that we should be able to express to our fellowmen.

The First Attribute Is that of Patience

The King James Version of the Bible uses the term *longsuffering,* which I think better captures the idea than the term *patience*. The idea is "suffering long" in various situations in our lives. Someone said, "Patience is love expressed under pressure (courageous endurance)." I think you will agree that we live in an impatient age. We desire instant gratification in almost everything. Most of us do not like to wait. I know I struggle with this and need to be more patient. I have a difficulty with the way most people drive their cars. They are either driving too fast or too slow for me.

I am constantly blowing my horn at them. My wife is continually trying to get me to control my impatience, so she recently taped a label on the dashboard of our car that reads, "Do good to those who annoy you." Believe it or not, this has helped me. But how much better if I learn to listen to the Spirit within me. Patience also means "courageous endurance without quitting." This is God's attitude toward us, and we should do the same to others. Patience is a fruit of the Spirit that expresses the attitude both to others and events. William Barclay, in his book **Flesh and Spirit,** says, ***"It expresses the attitude to people which never loses patience with them, however unreasonable they may be, and which never loses hope for them, however unlovely and unteachable they may be. It expresses the attitude to events which never admits defeat, and which never loses its hope and its faith, however dark the situation may be, and however incomprehensible events may be, and however sore the chastening of God may be"*** *(91).*

God's patience is the sinner's only hope, because God is gracious and merciful, slow to anger, and His love is steadfast. This is demonstrated in **2 Peter 3,** as Peter writes of the last days and the pending day of the Lord, when final judgment will come. Unfortunately, instead of pleading the mercy and grace of God, people will listen to the scoffers and continue following their evil ways, believing there is no evidence that God is going to bring such a judgment. Peter, however, points out that they deliberately refuse to recognize the evidence of God's past judgment of the time of Noah and the flood **(II Peter 3–6).** Remember, God gave that generation 120 years to make up their minds to accept the offer of escape from His judgment. Peter writes, ***"The Lord is not slow in keeping His promises, as some understand slowness. He is patient with you not wanting anyone to perish, but everyone to come to repentance. But the day of the Lord will come"*** **(II Peter 9, 10).** As I have reflected on my years of pastoral ministry and as a college professor, I realized the importance of the virtue of patience. The preacher and the teacher must never lose faith in people, however unresponsive they may seem to be, and must never allow himself to despair. No one can preach or teach without patience. ***2 Timothy 4:2 says, "Preach the Word; be prepared in season and out of season; correct, rebuke and encourage with great patience and careful instruction."*** I have been rewarded many times in seeing individuals that

I struggled with, subsequently had patience with, and encouraged, to witness how God was able to put them in positions of leadership. This is a great virtue for any leader and disciple of the Holy Spirit, since it displays the very character of God.

The Second Attribute Is that of Kindness or Goodness

Kindness and goodness are closely connected words. Kindness is love in little acts; goodness is love in action. I am reminded of the words of the prophet Micah when he was dealing with Israel's mere formality and hypocrisy in their worship to God. They lacked true righteousness in the heart. Micah therefore spelled out what God required: *"He (God) has showed you, O man, what is good. And what does the Lord require of you? To act justly and to love mercy and to walk humbly with your God" (Micah 6:8).* In other words, your accepted worship practices are to be the result of simple faith, doing good to others, and walking humbly before God. There are many examples of the fruit of goodness being exercised. One of the great examples is found in the parable of the Good Samaritan in **Luke 10:30–36.** A man on his way to Jericho was robbed, beaten, and left to die. Both a priest and a Levite passing that way refused to help this poor man, showing indifference. This should have been a natural act of kindness from these religious men to do good. However, a Samaritan coming upon this scene immediately took pity and tended fully to this man's needs. We need to be reminded that Jesus told this parable in answer to the question of an expert of the law, "Who is my neighbor?" We should view anyone who has a need as our neighbor and be willing to show them kindness and goodness. It was said of Jesus, *"He went around doing good and healing all who were under the power of the devil, because God was with Him"* **(Acts 10: 38).** Let me summarize how this triad of virtues works together:

Patience (longsuffering) focuses our attention on restraint the ability of self-control, regardless of circumstances that may irritate. Our English use of the term "patience" tends to be directed toward all kinds of non-personal matters (e.g., a traffic light or waiting in line), However, in Paul's use, it is always used in contexts involving one's "forbearance" toward others. This better describes God's attitude toward human arrogance.

Kindness is the idea of moral goodness that enables a person to be friendly and kind toward others. The Scripture says, ***"Be kind and compassionate to one another, forgiving each other just as in Christ God forgave you"*** **(Ephesians 4:32).** Kindness is awareness of how the other feels and adapts one's attitude accordingly. It expresses itself in little acts of kindness.

Goodness, as we mentioned earlier, is closely allied with kindness. Goodness has a more all-embracing quality, describing one's character. Believers are described by Paul: ***"I am convinced, my brothers, that you yourselves are full of goodness"* (Romans 15:14).** In another place, Paul says, ***"Let us do good to all people"*** **(Galatians 6:9, 10).** In the Book of Acts, we are introduced to Barnabas as ***"A good man, full of the Holy Spirit and faith"* (Acts 11:24).** His goodness was recognized by fellow believers in that they changed his name from Joseph to Barnabas, which means "one who comes alongside" **(Acts 4:36–37; 9:23–27; 11:20–31; 13:1–3; 15:35–41).**

Life in the Spirit expressed in personal virtue: *Faithfulness, Meekness, and Self-Control*

Finally, there are three virtues which have to do more directly with a disciple of the Spirit as an individual. What we do as individual Christians is very important to our modeling Christ in our world of influence, such as our work, our family and relatives, our church, and our neighbors.

The Virtue of Faithfulness. Our faithfulness to God should express itself toward others. It also carries the idea of integrity, honesty, and loyalty. Christianity has suffered much from Christians who did not exercise this to the world. Faithfulness is reflected in our integrity before God and others.

"After His Sunday messages, the pastor of a church in London got on the trolley Monday morning to go back to his study downtown. He paid his fare, and the trolley driver gave him too much change. The pastor sat down and fumbled the change and looked it over, counted it eight to ten times. And you know the rationalization, 'It's wonderful how God provides.' He realized he was tight that week and this was about what he would need to break even, or at least enough for his

lunch. He wrestled with himself all the way down that old trolley trail that led to his office. And finally he came to the stop and he got up, couldn't live with himself, walked up to the trolley driver, and said, 'Here, you gave me too much change. You made a mistake.' The driver said, 'No, it was no mistake. You see, I was in your church last night when you spoke on honesty, and I thought I would put you to the test'" (Paul Lee Tan, Encyclopedia of 7,700 Illustrations).

We would be surprised how many people around us are watching our lives and actions without our knowledge. I am reminded that, while attending seminary, I was able to provide my expenses by driving a taxi cab in the afternoon and evening hours. I was hired by a man who was a member of the church I was attending and who owned the cab company. He was reluctant to dispatch me to certain places, like bars or possible crime areas, since I was a minister and seminary student. Because of his overly protective attitude, I was always dispatched to rather local areas, and the cab fees and tips were very meager. As a result, I was having financial difficulty. One evening, I picked up a fare who was very intoxicated, and I had a difficult time handling him. We arrived at the hotel where he was registered, and I escorted him to his room and got him settled. When I returned to the taxi cab, I was shocked to see a large roll of money with a heavy rubber band around it where he had been sitting. I assumed it belonged to this passenger. As I observed this large amount of money, my conscience went into a time of debate as I reasoned, *This would really help me to meet my financial need. Who would know? The man was drunk he probably wouldn't remember.* However, the Holy Spirit quickened my mind to my need to be honest and faithful to God and this man. I immediately went back into the hotel and to the man's room to awaken him, which took quite awhile. He came to the door, and I asked him if he was missing any money. He went inside to check his belongings and rushed back, saying, "Yes! Yes! Did you find it?" He described the roll of bills and told me it was money he collected for the company where he was employed. As I handed him the money, he embraced me and pounded my back, repeating, "Thank you! Thank you!" As a result, he gave me a large tip for my honesty. My fellow cab drivers thought I was crazy not to keep the money, but it gave great respect to my faith and character, and it provided an open door to witness to them. They gave me the title "Yellow Cab Chaplain." It is so important to be a faithful and honest servant for God.

The Virtue of Meekness This is probably the most misunderstood virtue mentioned in Scripture. Earlier versions translated it ***gentleness.*** Jesus speaks of Himself being gentle and humble in **Matthew 11:29**: *"Take my yoke upon you and learn from me, for I am gentle and humble in heart, and you will find rest for your souls."* Jesus commends Himself as a teacher who is meek (gentle) and humble (lowly) unlike like the rabbis, who were hard and haughty. Their yoke of endless ceremonial demands and formal duties were heavy burdens. Jesus invites these toiling ones to come and take His yoke that is easy (well-fitted), and they would find, rest, peace, security, fellowship, and eternal life. Notice He says, "Come, take my yoke" and "learn about Me," and you will understand and experience the kingdom of God. It is interesting to note that in Bible days, many farmers created so-called "uneven yokes." These yokes had a small side and a large side. This was so they could utilize both a strong animal (ox) on the larger side and a weaker animal on the smaller side (e.g., a donkey). Spiritually speaking, Jesus is saying, "Take my yoke upon you, and I will take the heavy side of the yoke." What does this mean in terms of the fruit of meekness? It means that a disciple of the Holy Spirit will experience the Spirit's fruit of meekness, reflecting that same disposition of Christ to others. The apostle Paul speaks to this attitude in **Ephesians 4:1–3**: *"As a prisoner of the Lord, I urge you to live a life worthy of the calling you have received. Be completely humble and gentle (meek); be patient, bearing with one another in love. Make every effort to keep the unity of the Spirit through the bond of peace."* It denotes a patient endurance of wrongs, contentedness, quietness, and a tendency to be modest. It should be made clear that meekness does not carry the idea of weakness. Jesus said, *"I am meek and lowly in heart" (Matthew 11:29)*, and it was said of Moses that he was very meek; yet no one could accuse either of them as being weak. Meekness consists of the right way to use power and authority; it is power under control. It requires faith and courage.

The Virtue of Self-Control In a department store, a young husband was minding the baby while his wife was making a purchase. The infant was wailing, but the father seemed quite controlled and unperturbed as he quietly said, "Easy now, Albert, control your temper." A woman passing by remarked, "Sir, I must congratulate you! You seem to know how to speak to a baby." "Baby nothing!" came his reply. "My name is Albert!"

Many times we give the impression that we have self-control on the outside, but inside, we are straining to keep from exploding. When we consider our strength to be self-controlled, most of the time we discover we are weak. However, in Christ there is strength to control oneself. Consider the dilemma described by Paul in **Romans 7:14–24.** Paul was trying to do the will of God to the best of his ability, but he found that only having the law to govern his life was not enough. Even though he delighted in the law of God, he realized that there was another law waging war against his mind, making him a prisoner to the law of sin. Paul cries out in desperation, "What a wretched man I am! Who will rescue me from this body of death?" Then, suddenly, he realizes that Christ and the Holy Spirit are the answer to his dilemma! Gordon Fee in ***Paul, the Spirit and the People of God,*** points out aptly "That this last word (virtue) is unique because it does not appear elsewhere in Scripture with reference to the character of God. It is clearly aimed at the individual believer. This is not something one does in community; it is a general stance toward excesses of various kinds. It is in contrast to the rest of the terms in the list, which take aim at those eight works of the flesh that have to do with relational breakdowns, this one takes aim at either (or both) the sexual indulgences that appear as the first three works of the flesh (sexual immorality, impurity, debauchery) or (and) the excesses with which that list concludes (drunkenness, orgies). This too, is the effective working of the Spirit in the life of the believer" **(22, 23).**

Jesus was a great example for us concerning self-control. You might immediately say, "But He was the perfect man; why wouldn't He be able exercise control?" We should not be too quick to make this judgment. Jesus came into human flesh to identify with us in our humanity. Remember, the Scriptures state that He was tempted in every way, yet without sin **(Hebrews 4:15).** He can sympathize with us in all our weaknesses. Jesus demonstrated self-control in the power of the Holy Spirit. In **Luke 4: 1-12** tells us that following His baptism in the Jordan and being full of the Holy Spirit, He was led into the desert and tempted by the devil. He experienced temptation in all three areas that the apostle John mentioned in **I John 2:15–17** concerning the world system. ***"Do not love the world*** *or anything in the world. For everything in the world the lust (craving) of the flesh, the lust of the eyes, and boasting what one has or does."* The devil, realizing that Jesus was very hungry following a forty-day fast, tempted Him to create bread out of stones to satisfy His flesh. Jesus controlled this desire and said, *"It is written man does not live on bread alone(Luke 4: 2-4)"* Then he led Jesus to a high place and showed Him all the kingdoms of the world and said, *"Worship me, and I will give you all their authority and splendor, for it has been given to me and I can give it and I can give it anyone I want to.(Luke 4: 5-7)."* I would like to imagine that Jesus, looking at all these kingdoms, prompted a smile on His face and inwardly was saying, "Don't you know My Father and I created these?" Jesus said, *"It is written: worship the Lord your God and serve Him only.(Luke 4: 8)." Then the devil led him to Jerusalem and had Him stand on the highest point of the temple. He urged Jesus to prove that He was the Son of God by throwing Himself down from there. The devil quoted the scripture that declared that Jesus would have the protection of angels. Again, Jesus revealed self-control and said, "Do not put the Lord your God to the test!(Luke 4: 9-12)."* The devil left, because he was no match for the power of the Holy Spirit, who gave Jesus self-control. It may be, therefore, that self-control puts the finishing touch on the list of virtues which are mentioned in connection with the conflict that rages between "the flesh" and "the Spirit" in **Galatians 19-21.** All these virtues listed by Paul in **Galatians 5:22, 23** were to be found in Jesus Christ as He walked on earth. Therefore, to bear the fruit of the Spirit is to live a Christlike life made possible as disciples of the Holy Spirit. Paul has been speaking of freedom from the law, and he closed this list of virtues with the statement, "Against such things there is no law." Of course there is no law against such virtues! Let us be reminded that the character of Christ is revealed through the indwelling of the Holy Spirit as He operates through the body of believers as disciples of the Spirit.

Chapter Six

DISCIPLES OF THE HOLY SPIRIT: THE GIFTS DIMENSION

In order to be able to function as disciples of the Holy Spirit, there should be a comprehensible understanding not only the fruit of the Spirit, but also of the gifts of the Spirit . This chapter and those to follow constitute the heart and purpose of this book. Several years ago as I was doing an extensive study on this subject, I discovered an interesting pattern or structure in the Old Testament that was reflected in the New Testament structure of the gifts of the Holy Spirit. The following chart will help you understand the unity that exists between the Old Testament and the New Testament and the purpose of the gifts of the Holy Spirit as we proceed in our study.

The Old Testament structure reflected in the New Testament

OLD TESTAMENT	Observation	NEW TESTAMENT
Israel's Corporate Body	(Both seen as unified people)	The Church as the body of Christ
Prophetic Gift	(Many have gifts but not office)	Motivating gifts (Romans 12:5–8)

Prophetic Office	(Those who have gifts and office)	Office gifts (Ephesians 4:11)
To Build Up the Nation	(NT gifts build up Church)	Manifesting gifts (I Corinthians 12)
Israel Represents God's Character	(Believers reveal Christ's character)	Fruit of the Spirit (Galatians 5)
Israel Represents God's Power	(NT Church reveals God's power)	Gifts of the Spirit (I Corinthians 12)

As we move into this particular dimension, I am fully aware of the controversies and various teachings concerning the gifts of the Holy Spirit. In fact, that is the reason I have embarked on writing on the subject. For many years, I have struggled with the lack of discipline and knowledge that has accompanied the ministries that focused on the supernatural manifestations of the Holy Spirit.

It seemed to me that there has been an attempt to revive the fullness of the Spirit that characterized the early church. I certainly would agree that the church today needs a fresh outpouring of the Holy Spirit and His anointing to break through the growing secularization of the church and society that is controlling much of the thinking and actions today. However, even though the motive seems right, there is the danger of over extending and embellishing beyond Scriptural boundaries. There is the tendency to think that one can control the action of the Holy Spirit to their bidding, much like the vending machine mentality. I have faced criticism during part of my ministry because of my emphasis on maintaining balance and sensitivity to the person of the Holy Spirit. Recently I discovered R. T. Kendall's book, entitled ***Sensitivity of the Spirit: Learning to stay in the flow of God's direction.*** Dr. Kendall's insight and explanations as to how we both please and grieve the Holy Spirit is the best I have ever read and should be a must-read for pastors and congregations. We are living in a crude and vulgar age, and not much is considered sacred anymore. I am deeply concerned that in our endeavor to be relevant to the present culture, we are insensitive to the ministry and person of the Holy Spirit in trying to develop our so-called "contemporary" worship programs. Much of the confusion and the misuse of the gifts of the Spirit are due to not giving priority to the fruit of the Spirit as the governing principle in the operation of the gifts of the Spirit. They must not be separated, but rather integrated, as we will see in later chapters. The gifts of the Holy Spirit manifested in the ministry of Jesus Christ and integrated into the lives of His disciples become the legacy of our Lord to the Church through the dispensation of the Holy Spirit. Thus, by the integration from Jesus through His immediate disciples to the post-resurrection church, the power and gifts of the Holy Spirit continue to manifest the character and workings of God on earth.

There has been a lack of ethical quality in the practice of the gifts of the Holy Spirit among the body of believers. I am convinced that we need to concentrate our efforts toward developing discipleship based upon the understanding that to walk in the Spirit is to be disciples of Jesus through the Holy Spirit. There are those who may question the use of the term ***disciple*** here rather than ***believer,*** since the term ***disciple*** is not used in the epistles. However, keep in mind that the Gospels and Acts, with an abundant use of the term ***disciple***, were written after many of the epistles. The idea continues to be crucial in the epistolary literature. The concept is so much a part of the fellowship that it is assumed, and the ideas of this disciple band with its interaction are part of the whole New Testament. The New Testament pattern of discipling and discipleship revolves around the structure of the body and interacting discipleship. It is a discipling community with diversity of gifts, diversity of functions, and mutual edification with a commission to build up the body of Christ. Few commands of our Lord weigh on our Christian consciences as much as the Great Commission of **Matthew 28:18–20.** It is little wonder that we feel compelled to engage in some kind of discipleship program based upon the last words of our Lord: ***"All authority in heaven and on earth has been given to me. Therefore go and make disciples of all nations, baptizing them and teaching them to obey everything I have commanded you. And surely I am with you always, to the end of the age."***

It appears to me that the idea should extend to our present undisciplined day. Let us continue toward understanding how the gifts, properly understood, develop a disciplined and effective church to be a catalyst to demonstrate God's wisdom and glory. The various gifts are found in several places in the New Testament epistles: **Romans 12:6–8; I Corinthians**

12:8–11, 28; Ephesians 4:11; and I Peter 4:11. We will deal with each of these areas in the order listed.

The Motivating Gifts of Grace, I Corinthians 12: 6-8

One of the most helpful things about Paul's letters is that he follows a definite pattern in his writings. The first parts of his epistles generally deals with doctrinal or theological issues, and in the second parts, he shifts to practical instruction and application of those doctrinal and theological issues. This is evident in his letter to the Romans. **Romans 1–8** deals with God's plan of salvation and righteousness for all mankind, Jew and Gentile alike (**Romans 1:16, 17**). The theme of the letter is, **"A righteousness from God."** Chapters 9–11 are considered a parenthesis, rehearsing the righteousness of God as applied to Israel's past, present, and future. When we come to **chapters 12–16**, Paul picks up from issues of **chapters 1–8** and expounds how righteousness is practiced. Paul never stopped with doctrine; he always hastened to apply the truth of the gospel to the specific details of life. In a sense, Paul was proposing, "How can the Christians function as the body of Christ in Rome?" This is a good, probing question for every Christian and church body today.

Paul said, first, *"I urge you, brothers, in the light of God's mercy, to offer your bodies (total personality) as a living sacrifice"* (**Romans 12:1**). The kind of conduct being called for is not possible for just anybody. The only people who are ready for this appeal are those who have heard and found the gospel as *"the power unto salvation"* and vowed to be disciples of the Holy Spirit, *"holy and pleasing to God"* that is, separated unto God. If we are truly disciples who have experienced the benefits of Christ's atonement, then it's only reasonable that we would put ourselves absolutely at God's disposal. Our bodies, which were once controlled by sin, now are put in the hands of God for righteousness.

Secondly, Paul says to direct your attention to your lifestyle*: "Do not conform any longer to the pattern of this world (literally, to this age)" (Romans 12: 2)*. To be conformed suggests the gradual process by which the J. B. Phillips translation says, *"don't let the world around you squeeze you into its mold."* The world demands conformity. Our culture continues to become more and more ungodly, and it permeates every area of life. II

Timothy 3:1–5 says, *"But mark this: There will be terrible times in the last days. People will be lovers of themselves, lovers of money, boastful, proud, abusive, disobedient to parents, ungrateful, unholy, without love, unforgiving, slanderous, without self control, brutal, not lovers of good, treacherous, rash, conceited, lovers of pleasure rather than lover of God having a form of godliness but denying the power."*

How do we avoid this conformity? Paul continues, *"but be transformed by the renewing of your mind"* **(Romans 12:.2)**. It is interesting that the word *transform* is the Greek word *metamorphosis*, which means *"to undergo a complete change from one form into another."* This change, under the power of God, will find expression in character and conduct. It is a change from within by the power of Christ's love. With our minds transformed, we see the futility of the present world and its way of life. It is through this process of offering our total personality to God, determining not to be conformed to this world's system, and allowing the transformation of the way we think and act that we are to direct our attention to our role in the body of Christ, His church. You and I need to discover where we belong in the body of Christ. What motivating gift of grace do we have to minister and serve? In **Romans 12:3–8** we are given the revelation of these gifts. It is important to understand that unity within the body of Christ is always the focus.

The Seven Motivational Gifts of Grace and their Functions (Romans 12:3–8)

As a disciple or believer experiencing a renewed mind, the focus will now be directed toward community life. Each must take stock of his or her gift and its benefit of the community.

As Paul begins to elaborate on these gifts, he gives some preliminary directives:
1. Paul is speaking to them by virtue of his office as an apostle, given by God's grace **(v.3)**.
2. You must have an honest estimate of yourself. *"Do not think more highly of yourself than you ought to, but think soberly"*— think high enough, that is; don't underestimate (v. 3).

3. You must think with the measure of faith that God has given you in your gift **(v. 3)**.
4. All members do not have the same function. Like your human body, there is diversity **(v. 4)**.
5. We, being many, form one body and belong to each other **(v. 5)**.

It is important that the various gifts of the Spirit be understood within the context they are mentioned in this case, the epistle to the Romans. There appears to be tension between Jewish and Gentile Christians in Rome concerning Gentile adherence to Jewish law, especially circumcision **(Romans 2:25–3:1; 4:9–12)**, Sabbath observance, and food laws **(Romans 14:1–23)**. Paul is emphasizing the importance of God's righteousness in that His righteous salvation issues right standing with God. This, in turn, should give both Jew and Gentile the attitude that unity is possible. This can be effected through the motivational gifts of the Spirit. The motivational gifts listed here in Romans 12 are directed toward ministry to each other within the body of Christ. Let us begin by looking at these seven spiritual gifts listed here.

All the following gifts are experienced to some degree, but you will recognize that one gift will be dominant and will be your source of motivation. The church as a body ministers, and each member has a function of ministry to one extent or another. The Christian must tend to his own sphere of ministry of grace given to him, neither begrudging others nor inflating his own position. I will attempt to give an explanation of each of these gifts and illustrate how they would possibly operate within the fellowship of believers. This attitude does not end in the ministry of the church, but reaches beyond to the civic domain and fellow citizens **(Romans 13)**.

The Motivational Gift of Prophecy Romans 12:.6)

Prophecy is the most frequently mentioned of all the gifts. It appears in all the various lists mentioned in the New Testament. There are three focuses on prophecy in God's word: the office **(Ephesians 4:11)**, public utterance **(I Corinthians 12:10; 14:1–5)**, and motivational **(Romans 12:6)**.

Motivational prophecy is defined as t**he special ability to perceive and communicate truth for understanding, correction, repentance,**

or edification. The gift of prophecy was bestowed upon the church as a whole **(Acts 2:16)**, but in particular measure upon certain individuals who were distinctively known as prophets. Only a few of the Christian prophets are mentioned—Judas and Silas **(Acts 15:32)**, the prophets at Antioch **(Acts 13:1)**, Agabus, and prophets from Jerusalem **(Acts 11:9)**. But I Corinthians reveals that there were several of them in the Corinthian church. Occasionally, some were empowered to make an authoritative announcement of the divine will in a particular case **(Acts 13:1)**. In rare instances, we find them uttering a prediction of a future event **(Acts 11:28; 21:10)**. However, ordinarily their message was one of edification, exhortation, and consolation **(I Corinthians 4:7)**. In the Romans context, prophecy is a ministering function and not a prophetic office. This is a person who tends to (1) confront and bring people to accountability—speaking the truth in love"; (2) identify, define, and hate evil; and (3) is concerned for the truth and reputation of the program of God. John the Baptist is a good example of this bold, confronting, and jealous for truth. There can be some dangers and misuses of this gift. Sometimes prophets can develop a negative, critical spirit and be insensitive to people. They can be intolerant of opinions and views that differ from theirs. They can be lacking in love and genuine concern for the person or situation.

The Motivational Gift of Serving (Romans 12: 7)

The Greek term is *diakonia*—the idea of doing practical things to help others. This is the same word that is used for *deacon*. This is a person who is motivated to (1) meet practical needs of others in love; (2) demonstrate love in deeds rather than words; (3) release the office gifts to do important tasks (in Acts 6, apostles chose seven deacons to serve in order that they could continue their preaching ministry); (4) see things done immediately and work well on short-term goals; and (5) be alert to needed tasks and serve behind the scenes. My widowed mother was that type of person. She was a faithful member of an upper-middle-class liturgical church. I was always disturbed as to how the church took advantage of her. She cooked and served meals for the church dinners. She did domestic work for many of the rather well-to-do parishioners. She was affectionately known as "Molly." However, they never considered her one of them. I used to say,

Disciples of the Holy Spirit

"Mother, why do you work so hard for the church and the people when they don't really treat us like one of them?"

She would just smile and say, "Son, we don't have much, but the church does provide some help for our welfare. You need to understand that I'm enjoying serving the Lord here, meeting the needs of others." I never forgot my mother's serving spirit and how she instilled the importance of serving in my brother and me. When my mother went to be with the Lord, I was overwhelmed at the great number of people from the church and the community came to the funeral to show their respect for Molly. Service is the backbone of the church. Jesus is the ultimate example of a server. He divested himself of his deity to become a man and serve **(Philippians 2:3–8)**.

Remember, just prior to His death, Jesus demonstrated the act of serving to His disciples by washing their feet **(John 13)**. There is a tendency for this person to over-commit and find it difficult to say no. They need to be responsive to the priorities of leadership instead of setting their own agendas. Sometimes they do consider themselves important to the kingdom. They need to esteem their gift, remembering that doing practical deeds is a spiritual contribution to the body of Christ. There's a danger of seeking praise for their tasks. Though the community needs and will give praise to them, praise should not be the motive.

The Motivational Gift of Teaching (v. 7)

The Greek term for teacher is ***didasko**—"to teach or give instruction."* This is a special ability that God gives to certain members of the body of Christ to communicate information relevant to the health and ministry of the body and its members in such a way that others will learn. This is not necessarily the official office of teacher. It could be a one-on-one situation, such as parents, a volunteer Sunday school teacher, or a mentor to certain people who need to be discipled. This type of person is motivated to pass on truth to others. (1) They love building believers in their understanding in order that they may maintain a healthy Christian life. (2) They love to explain details and interpret the Scriptures. (3) They are disturbed when texts are taken out of context and desire the accuracy of words. (4) They devote themselves to seeking God and His Word. (5) They show great enthusiasm for revealed truth. Every church should discern those in the congregation who seem to have this gift. The Christian Education department should be open to allow people who have this motivation to have an opportunity to test their ability. It would be wise to apprentice them with a seasoned teacher rather than assign them to a class position. The gift must be sufficiently used to know what it is and how it functions. There are also the possibility of some dangers and misuse of this gift. People with this gift have the tendency to be prideful of their Biblical knowledge and understanding.

The Motivational Gift of Exhortation (v. 8)

This is an interesting term in the Greek text. It is *paraklesis*, meaning *"a calling to one's side to aid them"* (*para* = **alongside** and *klesis* = **calling**). It is interesting that the Holy Spirit is called the *paraklete*; that is, He is one who comes alongside the believer. This gift is exercised to comfort or admonish in terms of some trial being experienced. An exhorter is not just one who is on the sidelines, but is one who is there with us, encouraging and helping us. They motivate others to their best effort—the highest level of being in Christ. If you stop to think about it, all scripture is actually an exhortation, admonition, or encouragement for the purpose of strengthening and establishing the believer in the faith. It is the capacity to urge people to action in terms of applying scriptural truth or encourage or comfort with scriptural truth. God is referred to as *"the God of all comfort"* in **II Corinthians 1:3, 4:** *"Praise be to the God and Father of our Lord Jesus Christ, the Father of compassion and the God of all comfort, who comforts those in any troubles, so that we can comfort those in any trouble with the comfort we ourselves have received from God."* The apostle Paul, in writing to the church at Colosse to encourage them, writes, *"Tychicus will tell you all the news about me. He is a dear brother, a faithful minister and fellow servant in the Lord. I am sending him to you for the express purpose that you may know about our circumstances and that he may encourage your hearts"* (**Colossians 4:7, 8**). No doubt the people of the church were concerned about Paul in his imprisonment, so he sent Tychicus along with Onesimus to exhort and comfort them that he was doing fine.. He also let them know that several people were there to comfort and encourage him in his confinement , such as Mark, Aristarchus, Epaphras, Luke, and Demas (**Colossians 4:10–12**). A great example of this gift is seen in the person of Barnabas, a name given to him by the apostles, which means "Son of Consolation" **(Acts 4:36)**. He came alongside Paul at a crucial time of his life when he tried to meet with the disciples but they were afraid to trust his conversion **(Acts 9:26–28)**. He complimented Paul's teaching gift and got him going in ministry **(Acts 11:22–26)**. He later came alongside John Mark when the apostle Paul refused to take him on his missionary endeavor. In fact, it resulted in a sharp disagreement, and Barnabas parted company with Paul. He and Mark went to Cyprus, and Paul chose Silas and went to Syria and Cilicia **(Acts 15:36–41)**. His encouragement to Mark not to quit eventually resulted in Mark writing his gospel. I have always been fascinated with Barnabas in that he is a great example of what it means to be a disciple of the Holy Spirit. There are others, of course, but his life demonstrates the importance of discipleship being a strong focus in the church today.

The Motivational Gift of Giving (Romans 12: 8)

The gift of giving is a special ability God gives to certain members of the Body of Christ to contribute their material resources to the work of the Lord with liberality and cheerfulness. Generally, these persons also seem to have the ability to earn money. This certainly does not mean that they are the only ones responsible for giving, because the entire church is admonished to give. In my years of ministry, I have had occasions where I witnessed this gift being executed to the glory of God. There were two Christian businessmen, Carl and Demos, both in the dairy business, who took an interest in the church planting for which I was commissioned. The first brother, Carl, made a sizeable pledge toward our building project, which allowed us to move forward in a short time. However, one day he awoke to discover that his huge dairy was almost completely destroyed by fire. I'll never forget how he responded to this tragedy. He said, "This dairy was not my business; it was given to the Lord long ago, and I am confident that He will take care of it."

Later that week, he called me and said, "Pastor, I don't want you to be concerned about the pledge I made to the church. I made that pledge, and it will be met." The pledge was met, because he put God first. His insurance company informed him that his losses would be completely covered. He rejoiced, because he was not aware that he had that coverage. He would have kept his promise, even if the insurance was not there.

The other businessman was not someone I knew personally, but I knew of him as a prominent Christian businessman in the area. Our church building was not quite finished, and the congregational pledges were not being met. The first payment was due on the bank loan we had made, and there was not enough money to pay it. The church board suggested that I go to the bank and inquire if they would let us pay the interest until we could acquire additional pledge money. I was embarrassed to have to do this, because it was a bad testimony of our commitment to the bank. When I entered the bank, the president motioned for me to come to his office. I thought the worst. When I sat down, he said, "Pastor, I don't know how to tell you this." I was expecting bad news. "I can't tell you who did this, but your church loan payments are taken care of for one year." I left the bank rejoicing and could hardly wait to announce this from the pulpit to the congregation. As I pondered this, I realized that this problem was the result of the congregation not keeping their pledge commitments. That next Sunday, I admonished the congregation that because they failed in their commitment, the Lord had to move upon an outsider to meet our obligation. The congregation responded in repentance, and they began to meet their pledges. Approximately two years later, the bank manager asked if I ever discovered who had paid our loan for one year. I told him I didn't have a clue. He said, "I think I can tell you now. It was a man named Demos, a prominent businessman in our community."

These incidents reveal several characteristics about the gift of giving for us to consider: (1) They were not motivated to give by emotional appeals. I believe if people would give to the Lord thoughtfully and consistently, there would be little need to give emotional appeals. (2) They inspired others to give because they believed in the mission of the church. It is unfortunate that when people are aware of so-called wealthy people in the congregation, they expect them to carry the load of the finances. Think about it. How many such people are part of a congregation? It is the obligation of the entire body of believers to give as God prospers them, and thus all are blessed. (3) They rejoice to know that they have had a part in answering prayer. (4) They give for the glory of God, knowing that what they possess belongs to God and that they are to be good stewards of what they have.

The Motivational Gift of Organization (Leader/Facilitator) (Romans 12:8)

The gift of organization is a special ability that God gives some members of the body of Christ to understand the immediate and long-range goals of a particular unit of the body of Christ and to devise and execute effective plans for the accomplishment of those goals. This gift can operate on any situation that needs to bring cohesiveness out of chaos. They have the ability to organize people, events, tasks, and manage details carefully and thoroughly. They have a deep satisfaction when everything fits together and runs smoothly. Great preachers are not necessarily great organizers. Good organizers do not necessarily make good preachers. That's why it is important to have people who are gifted in organization and administrative skills. They must have the ability to work with and through others. They have the insight to know who fits where. They should be able to take orders from those over them and not usurp authority that is not given to them. They generally can envision the finished project. Probably one of the great examples of the gift of organization and leadership in the Scriptures would be Nehemiah in the Old Testament and the apostle Paul in the New Testament. There are certainly some possible dangers and abuses in the use of this gift: (1) the danger of pride and misuse of power; (2) a lack of patience when things or people are not cooperating or are slow to catch on; (3) the tendency to drive themselves to the neglect of personal or family needs; (4) and having confidence in their own strengths and abilities, and not God's. This gift is highly needed in many areas of church life.

The Motivational Gift of Mercy (Empathy) (Romans 12: 8)

The gift of mercy is the special ability God gives to certain members of the body of Christ to feel genuine empathy and compassion for individuals, whether believers or unbelievers, who suffer in various ways with physical, mental, or emotional difficulties. They have ability to express God's love and concern for them. It's a gift that infiltrates other gifts, such as exhorting, prophecy, or teaching that may tend to lack empathy at times in their ministering. Some of the characteristics of the gift of mercy are: (1) the ability to discern and feel the atmosphere of joy or distress in an individual or group; (2) the desire to remove hurts and misunderstandings; (3) sensitivity and ability to avoid being firm or strict; (4) the ability to express love, grace, and dignity to those facing hardships or crisis; (5) the ability to serve others with extraordinary patience; (6) the ability to meet the emotional need of others; and (7) a desire to have Christians stop hating, bickering, and hurting one another. Jesus is the prime example of mercy and compassion in the Scriptures. He empathized with needs of the crowds as well as individuals who were cast down and dejected. Examples of biblical figures who had this gift are Dorcas in Acts 9:36 and the apostle John in I John, II John, and III John. Every Christian is expected to be merciful. This reflects the fruit of the Spirit.

I attended a seminar some years ago where Dr. Ed Hindson of Liberty University gave a verbal illustration of how the motivational gifts would operate in the church during a crisis situation. He used the imagery of person who was about to serve pie to a group at a table and suddenly tripped and dropped the pie. Hindson went on to use the incident of the dropped pie as an example of a crisis moment. I engaged one of my students, a gifted artist, to draw a series of pictures depicting the crisis of the dropping of the pie and how the problem was solved. . The illusrations on the following pages will depict how each of the motivational gifts would operate within the body of Christ in the time of crisis.

Here are several persons waiting to be served a delicious pie. Suddenly, the pie is dropped, creating a crisis for the host. How can there be a reasonable solution to the problem?

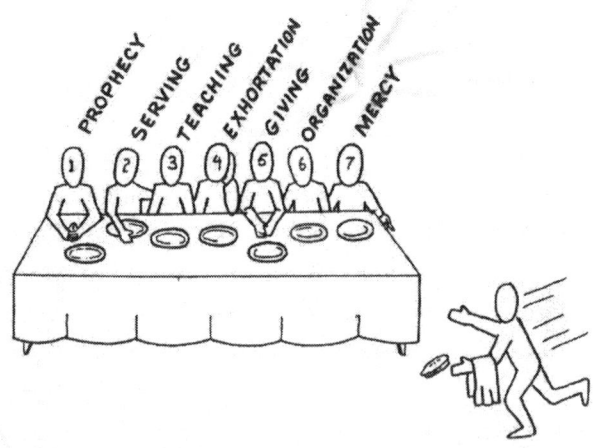

Disciples of the Holy Spirit

The person with the gift of prophecy would confront and bring to the person to accountability.

"You have failed in your duty to God and man. Your failure to be a good steward of this pie will bring you chastisement unless you repent. There are those whose appetite for pie will not be quenched because of your lack of responsibility!"

PROPHECY

The person with the gift of serving would take the initiative to offer their help to the situation.

"No wonder you dropped the pie; you had so much to do by yourself! Go get another pie while I clean up this mess better still, you just relax; I'll get another pie and serve it."

SERVING

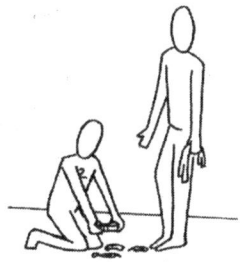

The person with the gift of teaching would analyze the situation and see if lack of instruction was the problem.

"Let's see if we can decipher the problem. The pie was probably not sufficiently cooled. A pie should be carried in both hands. You need to judge and measure your steps. Keep your focus on your destination

and don't hurry, especially as you near the table. Check the following: What kind of shoes are you wearing? Do you have hot pads? Do you pick up your feet or slide them?"

The person with the gift of exhortation would seek to comfort and encourage the person and not take it too seriously.

"Don't be overly concerned—it was just a pie; we probably didn't need it anyway. You could have hurt yourself, but thank God, it was only a pie, and it can be replaced. God still loves you, and He will help you to do better next time. Confess your weakness and ask Him for strength and wisdom and the ability to carry pies better. Can you feel His forgiveness? Take it by faith."

The person with the gift of giving desires to give quietly to produce effective ministry. They share spiritually as well as materially. They give to motivate others to give.

"You know, I think there is a more efficient way of doing this. Don't worry, I sent out for more pies. In fact, pastor, I would like to buy a pie-carrying cart so this problem will not happen again. However, I would appreciate it if you would not divulge who donated it."

The person who has the gift of organization tends to see the overall picture and take the lead and the challenge of getting things squared away. The person who has this gift has the ability to delegate and get people to help.

"Let's not get excited; the pie is not a complete loss. Let's get these plates over here. Hand me that serving tool. Okay, hold your plates down here. Let's see, if we take this piece carefully and divide that piece, we should be able to have somewhat of an equal distribution. Okay, form a line, get your portion, and go back to your table. Is everybody happy?"

The person with the gift of mercy discerns the atmosphere of joy or distress in individuals or groups. There is a great desire to remove hurts and show compassion.

"I know how you feel. I dropped a pie once—right in the lap of the host. It was awful; I cried for days. It's a terrible feeling, but God gave me grace, and I was able to get through it. I know you can, too!"

The motivational gifts help us to understand that every disciple of the Holy Spirit under the authority of Christ is to be a minister for Jesus within the body of Christ to maintain unity and strengthen the entire body for service and ministry to others. I recently came across a book entitled **When There's No Burning Bush** by Eddy Hall and Gary Morsch (Baker Books, 2004). The authors came to realize that ministry is not just for ministers. Many people may experience a sense of God calling them but become confused, thinking there has to be a "burning bush" experience or a "Damascus Road" encounter like the apostle Paul had. No doubt this misunderstanding has kept numbers of Christians from seeing themselves as ministers and fulfilling God's call. This is not an attempt to minimize the office gifts, such as the Pastor or teacher, that God gives as a more direct call. We need to recognize that the body of Christ is a living organism and not an organizational structure. The organizational image depicts a hierarchical pyramid that moves from top to bottom, from the highest function to the lowest. The church is an organism which consists of each part moving as a unit from one function to the other. This means that rather than being a program-driven ministry, it would be a call-driven ministry. When we are program-driven, the church generally consists of a few people who do everything, and the majority of the people remain idle. I trust by this time that you are becoming aware of my concern for a better understanding of the gifts of the Spirit and the importance of them operating within the scriptural patterns and not by fanatical whims that cause much misunderstanding and hinder the work of God.

The Office or Ministry Gifts of the Holy Spirit (Ephesians 4:11–16)

The motivational gifts create a concern and ministry to one another. However, they must be accompanied by caution to keep things in balance in the body of Christ. The so-called office gifts serve to supply such a balance. These gifts are recorded in **Ephesians 4:1–16.** Each book of the Bible has its own special theme and message, even though it may deal with many different topics. The theme of Ephesians is "the glorious church." All of Paul's epistles contain a beautiful balance between doctrine and duty, and Ephesians is a good example. In chapters 1–3, its doctrinal emphasis is our riches in Christ Jesus, and in chapter 4–6, our duties and responsibilities in Christ. It is in this fourth chapter that Paul urges the church to maintain its unity between the doctrine and the conduct or practice.

Paul says, *"I urge you to live a life worthy of the calling you have received"* (**Ephesians 4:1**). The word "worthy" is *axios,* which carries the idea having the same weight and takes the image of a weighing scale, where on one side is doctrine, and the other side is conduct. The point is that our conduct should be in balance with our doctrine (what we believe). We have a saying "practice what you preach" with this same idea in mind. The unity of the faith is very important to the health and witness of the church. We should keep in mind that the early church was becoming a mixture of Jews and Gentiles with different backgrounds, ideas, and lifestyles that could easily foster division. Therefore, the importance of having unity and maintaining it was essential. How is this to be accomplished? It is accomplished by the common faith that recognizes Jesus Christ as the head. We are the body and take on His character of humility, gentleness, patience, and love (**Ephesians 4:2**). Note that this relationship reflects the fruit of the Spirit that we discussed at length earlier. This unity called for is not uniformity. Unity comes from within and is a spiritual grace, while uniformity is the result of being under pressure from without. I like how Marvin Vincent, a Greek scholar, connects **Ephesians 4:4–6** as follows: *"I exhort you to unity, for you stand related to the Church, which is one body in Christ; to the one Spirit who informs it; to the one hope which your calling inspires; to the one Lord, Christ, in whom we believe with one common faith, and receive one common sign of that faith, baptism. Above all, to the one God, and Father"* (Kenneth S. Wiest, ***Ephesians and Colossians in the Greek New Testament,* 96**).

Let us now consider the office or ministry gifts, which are not so much "gifts" but actually gifted men that Christ placed in the church along with their purpose. The ministry of these gifted leaders is to prepare the individual saints (disciples of the Spirit) to do the work of the ministry and with a view toward building up the Church by winning the lost and adding to its membership which, in turn, will be equipped to do the work of ministry (**Ephesians 4:12**). The ultimate goal is for believers to reach unity in the faith. We are not to live in isolation, for after all, we are members of the same body (**Ephesians 4:13**). The members grow spiritually by feeding on the Word of God and ministering to each other. They are nurtured and gain maturity to be steadfast in the faith (**Ephesians 4:14**). They become disciples of the Spirit, expressing the character and power of Christ in the church and the world. How do these men, gifted by Christ, function within the body of believers? Let's consider these four offices or ministries:

The office or ministry gift of the apostle, which means *"one sent with a commission."* Jesus gathered many disciples (learners, followers) during His ministry and eventually selected twelve, designating them as apostles, and commissioned them to go forth as His representatives (**Matthew 10:1-4**). These men helped to lay the foundation of the Church (**Ephesians 2:20**), and some expositors believe that once this was accomplished, their ministry was no longer needed. Aside from the twelve specially appointed apostles, the Scriptures refer to a number of other apostles throughout the church. For example, Paul recognized James, our Lord's brother, as an apostle (**Galatians 1:19; I Corinthians 15:7**) along with Barnabas (**Acts 14:14**), Andronicus and Junias (**Roman 16:7**), and Silvanus and Timothy, who seem to be included as apostles in Paul's statement in **I Thessalonians 2:6**. However, there is no indication that as the original twelve began to die, they were replaced. But the gift of apostleship cannot be regarded as having been withdrawn with the death of the twelve apostles, since the term *apostle* can refer to anyone who is sent forth as a witness, particularly to establish churches. It is not uncommon to think of this office being executed in our present day missionaries. We must concede, however, that there are no apostles today in the strictest New Testament sense. The twelve were unique in their call and ministry. Those who continued to be recognized as apostles beyond the original twelve maintained the ministry function of spreading the gospel, planting churches, and preserving purity of doctrine. This helps to maintain unity outreach in the church. Its contribution to the building up of the body of Christ still continues, much like our modern-day missionaries.

The office or ministry gift of prophet.—Prophets seemed to be recognized in the early church, and at the same time, the gift of prophecy appeared to be a gift available to all believers without such a recognized position. In **Acts 2:17, 18**, the apostle Peter, speaking on the Day of Pentecost, proclaimed, *"'In the last days,' God says, 'I will pour out my Spirit on all people. Your sons and daughters will prophesy. Even on my servants, both men and women, I will pour out my Spirit in those days, and they will prophesy."* In the early church, there were two classifications of prophets. Any member of the body of believers who ministered, edified, exhorted, and comforted through the gift of prophecy was called a prophet (**I Corinthians 14:24, 31**). Another group, consisting of such men as Barnabas, Silas, Judas, Agabus, and others mentioned in **Acts 13:1**, were spiritual leaders of the church (**Acts 21:22**). While prophesy is more "forth-telling" than "foretelling," sometimes it may involve prediction of the future. The example is the two predictions of Agabus (**Acts 11:27, 28; 21:10–14**). The second prediction concerning Paul's soon-coming imprisonment in Jerusalem (**Acts 21:11**) did not cause Paul to change his plans. Agabus revealed only what Paul already knew (**Acts 20:22, 23**). The apostle Paul exhorted the Corinthian Christians to seek the gift of prophecy in preference to other gifts, especially in comparison to the function of the gift of tongues in the case of unbelievers being present in the church (**I Corinthians 14**).

To prophesy here was primarily *"inspirational utterances"* prompted by the Spirit for the edification of the believers. Basically, prophets were itinerant teachers who, under divine inspiration, instructed the church in Christian doctrine.

The office or ministry gift of the evangelist—"Evangelist" comes from the Greek word *euangelistes,* which is defined as "one who proclaims good news." The English word ***gospel* means "good news," from the Anglo-Saxon *god-spell*—a message from a god.** An evangelist, then, is one who devotes himself entirely to preaching the gospel, especially the good news of salvation through Jesus Christ. The term evangelist is used only three times in the New Testament **(Acts 21:8; Ephesians 4:11; II Timothy 4:5).** The clearest description of an evangelist is found in the ministry of Philip, who is specifically called an evangelist **(Acts 21:8).**

The following Scriptures in the Book of Acts give us characteristics of Philip's ministry and a pattern of New Testament evangelism. Philip preached the Word of God to the Samaritans, especially declaring the heart of the Gospel, which is Christ the Savior. "He preached Christ unto them" **(Acts 8:4, 5).** There were many who believed and were baptized as a confession of their faith **(Acts 8:12).** Mighty miracles of healing followed his preaching, and many were delivered from demon spirits The healing miracles gave greater effectiveness to Philip's ministry **(Acts 8:6, 7).** Philip was ready to witness about Christ as the Savior to whole cities or to one individual. Leaving Samaria, he was directed to the chariot of the treasurer of **Ethiopia (Acts 8:26), whom he led to Christ (Acts 8:35–38).** Philip's evangelistic ministry took him from city to city **(Acts 8:40)** (from N. M. Van Cleave and Guy Duffield, **Foundations of Pentecostal Theology,** 353). The evangelist's converts throughout the many areas of the country would no doubt gather with other believers and thus need to be discipled and nurtured. It was this need that fostered the gift of pastor and teacher.

The office gift or ministry of the pastor/teacher—The apostle, prophet, and evangelist constituted, for the most part, an itinerate form of ministry. Therefore, there was a need for local **and** more permanent ministry for the gathered believers in the church. In the grammatical structure of Ephesians 4:11, the term teacher does not have the definite article, as do the preceding terms for the ministry gifts. It seems, therefore, that teacher is to be taken together with pastor. It would seem that the words did not describe two classes of workers but two functions of one office. This does not mean that the terms are interchangeable. There may be teachers, such as mentioned in **Romans 12:7,** who are not pastors, but there cannot be pastors who are not teachers.

William Barclay, in his commentary on Galatians and Ephesians, made some very interesting observations concerning pastors and teachers. He believes that the pastor/teacher had the most important task in the whole church. This person did not travel as extensively as the apostles, prophets, and evangelists. He or she was generally established and did his or her work in one church body. He or she had extensive knowledge of the gospel story. Barclay points out that many people were coming to the church straight from heathenism and knew literally nothing about Christianity except that Christ captured their hearts. These teachers had to teach and explain the great doctrines of the faith **(174–175)**. These teachers were also pastors, and the word *pastor* in the Greek text is *poimen*—"shepherds." This gives us a better idea about the nature of their ministry. The one who shepherds God's flock is also a teacher of the Word, having both gifts of shepherding and teaching the flock. The duty of the pastor was to shepherd his flock and keep them safe. Jesus called Himself the Good Shepherd (**John 10:11, 14**). The writer of Hebrews refers to Jesus as the Great Shepherd of the sheep **(Hebrews 10:20)**. The word *pastor* itself is borrowed from animal husbandry, particularly sheep-raising.

We use the term as referring to the office of pastor that is, one who is the designated head of a local church. When we refer to the gift of the pastor, these are men that possessed special gifts given to equip all in the church, that by them, all believers would be equipped for the work of ministry. We have missed this truth for so many years in the church. Our churches today, in many cases, have become almost like corporations where the pastors are more like corporate executives with a number of paid staff that do all the work of the ministry. I have been encouraged by the number of books being published promoting the "simple church" concept today. The church needs to take a new look at its approach for reaching people. This is why I have been trying to share my understanding of the biblical concept of creating disciples of the Spirit who seek to be led by the Spirit and the Word of God. The Holy Spirit, in granting His gifts, distributes them wisely, so that the ministries of the church are appropriately portioned out to all the members of the body. This way, no one individual would be responsible for all the ministries at the same time. It is important that the equipping ministries of the church be kept separate from each other so that their functions can be effectively performed (Ephesians 4:11). It is obvious that the church has moved away from these scriptural directives and has changed from congregational or people-oriented ministry to a professional, leadership-program-oriented ministry.

Gilbert Bilezkian, in his book, ***Community 101***, made the following observation: ***"This gradual replacement of the priesthood of all believers by the ministry of a professional clergy has had disastrous consequences in two areas. The first is the disfranchisement of the laity from ministry. Awed by the elitist image projected by trained specialists, the average church member shrinks away from ministry involvements or reduces them to marginal supportive roles. The other is the devastating effect it has on the ministers themselves. The clergy-dominated system of doing church places on pastors the unrealistic burden of acting as if they were universally gifted so as to carry successfully the multitude of responsibilities that constitute the life of the local congregation"*** ***(155).***

We need to view the church as a body primarily as an organism in which each of its parts flow into each other and supply life and vitality to the whole body. However, we often view the church structured as a pyramid, with hierarchical levels moving from top to bottom. The leadership function begins with one person at the top. In contrast, leadership in the New Testament is always defined as plural. No one is ever designated as the single leader of a local church. Rather than visualizing the church ministries in pyramid form, visualize the pyramid as laid on its side, each gifted ministry flowing into each other. This gives balance to the church. Without this balance, the church will not grow as disciples of the Holy Spirit to maturity and unity. There clearly were leaders, but that leadership was not pyramidal; it was more horizontal in nature, and the leaders viewed themselves as servant leaders. Churches need to move toward establishing a productive ministry of equipping their congregation for ministry. There are too many idle Christians in the church who depend on paid staff and leaders to do the work of ministry. There needs to be revived effort to make disciples—who, in turn, will make other disciples. I remember when I first read the account of the day of Pentecost, I was not only struck with the disciple's experience of being baptized in the Holy Spirit, but also with the fact that they did not stay behind closed doors, but moved outside and challenged the people who had gathered. As the result of Peter's message, three thousand souls came to Christ, and the Church was born. How was it to function and grow? The chart on the next page gives a panoramic view of how the church should be people-oriented rather being program-oriented.

Programs or People?

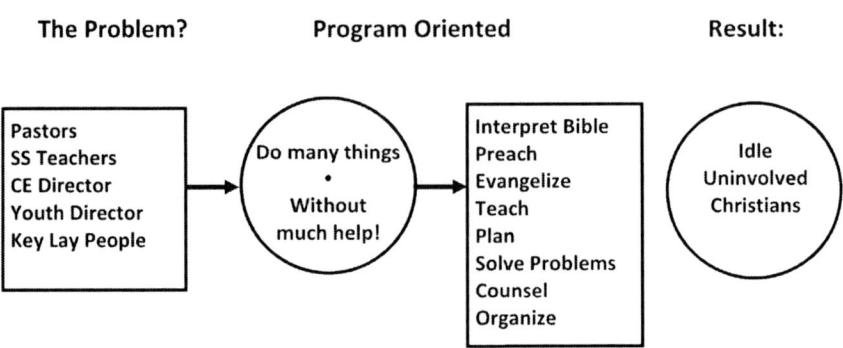

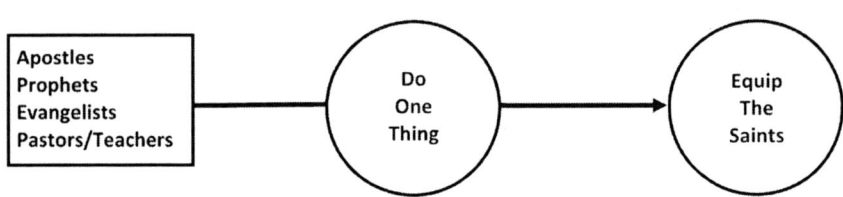

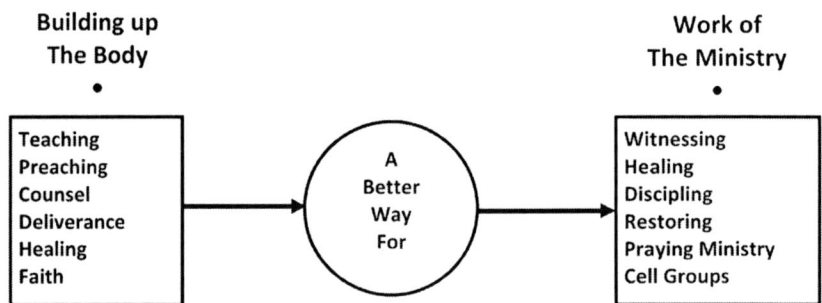

Chapter Seven

THE MANIFESTING GIFTS OF THE HOLY SPIRIT (I Corinthians 12–14)

The Apostle Paul's Concern for the Corinthian Church

The apostle Paul, in writing to the Corinthian church, was deeply troubled by the lack of ethical behavior in the total life of the church. Paul had received information concerning the conditions existing in the church from several sources, the household of Chloe being a primary source **(I Corinthians 1:11)** The main issue was concerning the divisions taking place as a the result of their carnal thinking and practices. Therefore, in the first half of the epistle **(I Corinthians 1–11),** Paul deals with the carnalities that have entered in and spoiled the witness and testimony of the Corinthian church. G. Campbell Morgan, in his book *The Corinthian Letters of Paul,* explains it this way: *"What were the carnalities? Divisions, derelictions from duty, difficulties in life, all caused by carnality. Those are the three movements in the first eleven chapters. When he turns to the spiritualities, he puts first, the unifying Spirit; secondly, the unfailing law of love; and thirdly, the Gospel of the resurrection triumph. Those three spiritualities will correct all the carnalities" (11).*

The Corinthian problem was a discipleship problem. The people had exchanged their loyalty from the compelling message of the cross for the words of men **(I Corinthians 1:17, 18)**. They had lost their single focus of following Christ together as a body of believers. They were divided as each said, "I follow Paul," another "I follow Apollos," and still another "I follow Cephas," and finally, those who said "I follow Christ" **(I Corinthians 1:12)**. This latter group appears to be legitimate on the surface, but how could Christ, who was no respecter of persons and a universal Savior, be formed into a separate party or division? This appears to be a self-righteous or holier-than-thou expression on their part. Because their focus was on human quality and ability, they were following a carnal way of thinking and acting. They were not acting as disciples of the Spirit, but rather as disciples of the flesh. However, the second half of the letter **(I Corinthians 12–16)** is directed toward spiritually corrective matters. In **I Corinthians 12:1**, Paul changes his focus by introducing spiritual matters" **(pneumatikon)**. Before Paul proceeded to deal with the gifts of the Spirit, he wanted them to understand that these gifts were activities initiated by the Holy Spirit and not by human abilities or talents. The nature of these spiritual gifts is that they focus on Christ and not the person(s) exercising them. In the first eleven chapters, Paul had been directing his attention to addressing those doctrinal issues that had been distorted due to their carnal, fleshly attitude as follows: actions in the church **(I Corinthians 1:10–4:21)**, moral problems **(I Corinthians 5:1–6:20)**, questions about marriage **(I Corinthians 7:1–40)**, limits of liberty **(I Corinthians 8:1–11:1)**, head covering in worship **(I Corinthians 11:2–16)**, and proper observance of the Lord's Supper **(I Corinthians 11:17–34)**.

Much of the confusion and rejection concerning the operation of the gifts of the Holy Spirit stems from not following Biblical mandates. I remember a certain evangelist conducting a tent meeting in which he claimed that at a certain time during the service, the Holy Spirit caused his hands to produce anointing oil. When this supposed miracle happened, he would ask people who needed healing to come forth for prayer. He would proceed to anoint them as long as the oil remained on his hands. There were those who claimed they received healing at that time. The tent meeting began to draw large crowds each night as news of this unusual gift spread across the area. Unfortunately, many people sitting in the

Disciples of the Holy Spirit

meeting were continually rubbing their hands, anticipating that oil would miraculously appear. Where was the focus? Apparently, not on Christ and the message. Sad to say, but this so-called miracle of oil appearing on the hands of the evangelist turned out to be a hoax. This is why we need to have clear Biblical directives so that we are not led by carnal or satanic influences that seek to discredit Christ and the Gospel.

I Corinthians 12–14 is very crucial to our understanding of manifestation of the Holy Spirit through His gifts. Many segments of the Church have considered this area of the gifts as irrelevant for today because of the completion of the Canon of Scripture. It is argued that these manifestations are not needed. These gifts were only temporary, to authenticate the Church and the gospel until the completion of the Canon. I find it difficult to embrace this proposed theory that dispensationalizes or compartmentalizes God's work to only a certain point in time. This kind of thinking has robbed the Church of needed power and made it skeptical of the manifestation of the Holy Spirit today. I know that the wholesale misuse of the Gifts of the Holy Spirit by charismatic individuals and movements through the years has contributed to such skepticism and mistrust. The basic Scripture used to argue the cessation of the gifts is I Corinthians 13:10: "But when that which is perfect has come, then that which is in part will be done away." The argument hinges on the meaning of the word *perfect*. The most acceptable is that perfection refers to when the Scriptures were completed as an accepted Canon (the collection of authentic books of the Old and New Testament considered inspired by God). However, there is no evidence that this is what is being referred to in I Corinthians 13:10. It is more feasible that it refers to the coming of Christ when what we now have partially will continue until we see "face to face" **(I Corinthians 13:12–13)**. The Corinthians misunderstood the manner in which the Holy Spirit works through individuals, and they abused the use of spiritual gifts. Therefore, Paul wrote to correct the situation by showing that there was a need for varied and multiple manifestations of the Spirit **(I Corinthians 12)**; the need for loving and unselfish motives in these manifestations **(I Corinthians 13);** and the need for self-control and for keeping an orderly, edifying manner in the church services **(I Corinthians 14)**. The church today should realize that Paul was not correcting the situation by doing away with the gifts. On the contrary, by the proper use of the gifts, the church would grow spiritually and promote the gospel to the world around them.

Three Guiding Principles which Determine a True Manifestation of the Holy Spirit (Corinthians 12:13)

"Now concerning Spiritual Matters" (I Corinthians 12:1) As we come to I Corinthians 12, Paul proceeds to deal with the situation in a constructive manner. It is obvious that many in the Corinthian church had come from paganism, and they were still evidently under the influence of the previous patterns of their former lives. Paul said that he did not want them to be ignorant concerning the operation of the Holy Spirit and His gifts in their lives. He proceeded to explain how one may know the true manifestation of the Holy Spirit. Paul gives three guiding principles that are also relevant to our understanding the ministry of the Holy Spirit. Let us consider Paul's three principles that determine the true manifestation of the Holy Spirit.

1. The Principle of Conscious Control (I Corinthians 12:2)

The thought of this verse is not difficult to grasp: "You were influenced and led astray by pagan powers" (idolatry/demonic). A believer in Christ will always have conscious control in the Holy Spirit **(I Corinthians 14:32–33, 40).** I have encountered numerous people through the years who register great fear concerning the experience of being filled with the Holy Spirit, thinking that they would experience some kind of a trance or uncontrollable state. Paul is explaining to these former pagan believers that "when you were pagans, somehow or other you were influenced and led away by mute idols" (I Corinthians 12:2). The sense of this sentence would be something like this: "When you were pagans, you were being misled by a power which continuously controlled you for the purpose of senseless idolatry." The point is, in sharp contrast, Christians under the power of the Holy Spirit always have conscious control. Unlike paganism, the Spirit of God does not, in the name of worship, force followers into wild, compulsive acts. The Holy Spirit's gentle, dove-like ministry is to strengthen their personalities through inspiration and not overpower in order to possess for fanatical demonstrations. We need to cautious of assigning certain behaviors as the work of the Holy Spirit. He can never be blamed for confusion (I Corinthians 14:32, 33) or things done in bad taste **(I Corinthians 14:40).** Never fear the ministry of the Holy Spirit in your life. He guides us into truth—the truth of Jesus Christ.

2. The Principle of Christ-Glorification (I Corinthians 12:3a)

There may have been blasphemous things said about Jesus Christ that occurred in pagan settings "inspired" by demonic spirits. However, Paul says, *"no one who is speaking by the Spirit of God says, 'Jesus be cursed.'"* This is a general rule meaning that if anyone, Jew or Gentile, whoever they might be, should blaspheme the name of Jesus, professing to be under the influence of the Holy Spirit, it is full proof that they are imposters. Why would Paul say this? Because the Holy Spirit in all instances would do honor to Jesus Christ, that is, glorify Him in all that He is and does **(John 16:13–15)**. It is possible and indeed probable that priests and priestesses of the pagan gods who pretended to be under the influence and inspiration might denounce the name of Jesus, because they would be opposed to His religion. Therefore, true disciples of the Holy Spirit would also bring honor and glory to Jesus under His influence and guidance.

3. The Principle of Creedal Faith (I Corinthians 12:3b)

Paul continues, "and no one can say 'Jesus is Lord' except by the Holy Spirit." While anyone can say Jesus is Lord, no one can say it from the heart except by the Holy Spirit in them. That is, He is Lord of my life, and all aspects of the Christian life stem from Him. The acknowledgement that "Jesus is Lord" was essentially the first Christian creed. The early church was called to live its life and maintain its testimony in tumultuous times. Christians were brought before Jewish authorities and Roman officials to attest their allegiance to Jesus Christ. Being brought before the Jewish tribunals did not result in any severe punishment, but rather hysterical outbursts of indignation and wrath. However, when brought before the Roman officials, that was a different matter. When they were required to make some attestation of supreme loyalty to Christ or Caesar, the

Christians confessed, "Jesus Christ is Lord, not Caesar," which resulted in punishment and persecution.

In comparing the Jewish tribunal with the Roman tribunal, we dare not minimize the suffering that occurred from both situations. The Jewish tribunal resulted in the shunning of people from the synagogues, as well as from their families, and they were treated as outcasts. On top of this, they suffered the cruelty of the Roman government, which included imprisonment, torture, and in many cases, death. Declaring "Jesus is Lord" is not to be taken lightly; there is a cost for such commitment. This process shaped and strengthened the Christian's unified confession of "Jesus is Lord."

Philippians 2:1–11 gives a good summary of what the Christian attitude should be. This needs to be our confession in our tumultuous times in this twenty-first century: **"Jesus is Lord!"** He must be in the forefront of our lives that are constantly striving to be self-reliant, self-assured, and independent. I am reminded of the wisdom of **Proverbs 11:2:** *"When swelling and pride come, then emptiness and shame come also; but with the humble—those who are lowly, [who have been pruned or chiseled by trial] and renounce self is skillful and godly Wisdom and soundness"* (AMP).

Manifesting Gifts (I Corinthians 12:4-30)

As we continue to consider what it means to be a disciple of the Holy Spirit, it is important to be aware of these guiding principles. They will be profitable in understanding the importance of the spiritual gifts within the body of Christ and maintaining Christian unity, which is our strength.

The understanding of these gifts and their operations is crucial for the church and those coming into the church and becoming members of the body of Christ. Remember that being disciples of the Holy Spirit requires discipline and maturity. Much too often, these gifts have not been taken seriously and have been exercised by groups and individuals without much sensitivity to their real meaning and purpose, thus giving a false representation of their true purpose for the body of Christ. Jesus instructed His original disciples and gave them opportunity to minister in His power. However, they were continually being disciplined toward maturity and wisdom so that their ministry for the kingdom would properly demonstrate the character and power of Christ. The same is true for the post-Pentecost disciples in continuing the ministry of Christ. I have observed in my years of ministry, especially among my Pentecostal and charismatic brethren, a lack of maturity. They are operating much like undisciplined children handling powerful things without knowledge. We must be very serious about what we have been given by the Holy Spirit. Here is empowerment that has great potential for good, but misused, it can do much harm. It would be like placing nuclear power in the hands of an untrained and immature person. As we have already observed, when nuclear power was discovered, its purpose was to be for the good of mankind. Though we have experienced many good things from this power, we, unfortunately, have seen its great destructive power. Today, it is creating great fear to our world, because nuclear power is in the hands of fanatical war mongers. We need mature disciples of the Spirit in the church today who understand these powerful, wonderful gifts so that the church may be edified and built up and can demonstrate the body of Christ as a strong tower and meaningful force in our world today. The church needs these gifts operating today as never before. However, there are few churches that are willing to search the Scripture honestly and openly concerning the ministry of the Holy Spirit. As we consider these manifesting gifts, the Apostle Paul helps us to understand that there are different kinds of gifts administration and operations. The following three verses (**I Corinthians 12:4–6**) reveal that these gifts come from the triune God: *"There are different kinds of gifts, but the same Spirit. There are different kinds of service, but the same Lord. There are different kinds of workings, but the same God works all of them in all men."*

Three Major Categories:

1. *Charismata* **(gifts)** (**I Corinthians 12: 4**) is actually anything freely given; the *source* of the manifestation is the endowment of grace by the Holy Spirit
2. *Diakonia* **(administration)** (**I Corinthian 12: 5**): the practice of the manifestations—any type of service, ministry, or work by the same Lord

3. ***Energemata* (operations, workings) (I Corinthians 12: 6)**: the ***effects*** of the manifestations the activity that calls forth miracles by the same God (Father)

It is interesting that Paul connects these three categories with the Godhead Spirit, Lord, and God. We can define these gifts as ***"certain powers given to persons freely to be manifested through ministry (office gifts and motivating gifts) to others for their edification and growth."*** There is an important key verse of this chapter that we dare not overlook as we begin to study these particular gifts. **I Corinthians 12:7** says, ***"Now to each one the manifestation of the Spirit is given for the common good". The Greek text uses sumphero***—literally, ***"to profit."*** This means that everything listed in this chapter is a manifestation of the Spirit and suggests that their purpose is to bring man to a higher end or a more useful purpose. Certainly it is for the mutual good of the church, not self-glorification. The things of the Spirit are not limited to some spiritual elite or professional ministry; they are intended for every member of the body of Christ. I have found this to be a serious problem in Pentecostal and charismatic churches. It is not unusual for a person to consider themselves specially endowed with a certain gift and tend to dominate a service by its manifestation, e.g., speaking in tongues and interpretation, not considering the total ministry of the service. Some even have been deluded into thinking that having a gift assumes greater holiness. The gifts are not designed to increase our sanctification or maturity in Christ; that's the ministry of the fruit of the Spirit. Much of this occurs because there is a lack of teaching, along with the church leader's so-called fear of quenching the Holy Spirit because of a lack of discernment of a true manifestation. The apostle Paul deals with some of this **I Corinthians 14.**

The Need for a Full, Varied, and Multiple Manifestation of the Gifts of the Spirit

The Nine Manifesting Gifts (I Corinthians 12:8–10)

For one to attempt to precisely define the various manifestations in this chapter is a difficult a task. There are numerous scholars who think it is quite possible that Paul did not intend that the nine gifts in this chapter would be taken for specific manifestations with clearly defined limits. We must grant the possibility that these gifts could be part of a longer continuum. This may not be so, but I will confine this study to what is already in the chapter and leave the speculation to others. It is not altogether clear if there is some logical order or grouping to these various manifestations. I have concluded in my study and teaching of these manifestations that there is a particular pattern that gives us a logical, practical understanding of what these gifts represent to the body of Christ in their operations. This helps us maintain a holistic view of the ministry of the Holy Spirit in the church. Let us consider the following overall groupings of these gifts, and then we will deal with each section individually and explain their functions directed toward the body of Christ.

Gifts of Revelation or the Mind of God

1. Word of wisdom
2. Word of knowledge
3. Discerning of spirits

Gifts of Power or the Power of God

1. Faith
2. Working of miracles
3. Gifts of healing

Gifts of Inspiration or the Voice of God

1. Prophecy
2. Different kinds of tongues
3. Interpretation of tongues

Let us rehearse again the purpose of the gifts. (1) The Holy Spirit distributes gifts to the body of believers in order that the ministry of Jesus Christ might continue **(John 14:12; Acts1:1, 2)**. (2) These gifts provide a supernatural order. Consider the extremes we would have without designated gifts. (3) These gifts are for building up the body of Christ (edifying the order) to create unity and harmony for ministry.

Dr. George P. Kimber

The Manifesting Gifts of Revelation

These particular gifts are associated with the mind of God and His thoughts, wisdom, intelligence, and omniscience (all-knowing). However, this does not mean that we will receive His full wisdom and knowledge. In **I Corinthians 1, 3,** the word *wisdom* is always used with a marked distinction between the wisdom of man and the wisdom of God (**I Corinthians 2:1–16, 3:18–23**). These manifestations coincide with the gifts directed toward the perfecting of the saints, which are the office gifts of **Ephesians 4:11. Deuteronomy 29:29** says, *"The secret things belong to the Lord our God, but the things revealed belong to us."* Isaiah 55:8, 9 says, *"'For my thoughts are not your thoughts, nether are your ways my ways,' declares he Lord. 'As the heavens are higher than the earth, so are my ways higher than your ways and my thoughts than your thoughts.'"*

We can only know what God deems to reveal to us.. Paul, in talking about the wisdom of God says, *"We speak of God's secret wisdom, a wisdom that has been hidden However, as it is written: 'No eye has seen, no ear has heard, no mind has conceived what God has prepared for those who love Him.' But God has revealed it to us by his Spirit. The Spirit searches all things, even the deep things of God. For who among men knows the thought of a man except the man's spirit within him? In the same way no one knows the thoughts of God except the Spirit of God"* (I Corinthians 2:7-1).

A Word of Wisdom *(Logos Sophias)*

This is not a gift of wisdom in general. It is not deep insight into Scripture or the ability to interpret Scripture. It is not the ability to speak wisely or tactfully. These could all be developed by natural means. Instead, like all the gifts, this is a supernatural revelation of the mind and purpose of God communicated by the Holy Spirit (generally in the future). The Old Testament prophets experienced this manifestation in receiving and writing their prophecies. **II Peter 1:20, 21** tells us, *"Above all, you must understand that no prophecy of Scripture came about by the prophet's own interpretation. For prophecy never had its origin in the will of man, but men spoke as they were carried along by the Holy Spirit."* You will note that it does not refer to this as **"the gift of wisdom"** but rather *"a word of wisdom" (logos sophias)*. This can be explained, for example, like that of a lawyer who, upon being summoned to defend a client, will extract from his vast knowledge of the law a word of wisdom that applies to this particular case. God gives a word of wisdom from His full wisdom to a certain situation communicated by means of the Holy Spirit. A few Scriptural examples would be: God giving the Law to Moses (**Exodus 20**), Joseph being given a revelation of his life (**Genesis 37**), and the apostle John on the Isle of Patmos (**Revelation 1**).

A Word of Knowledge *(Logos Gnoseos)*

This is a companion gift to wisdom, but again notice that it is not "the gift of knowledge" but *"a word of knowledge."* It differs from natural wisdom and knowledge. It is a supernatural revelation from God of any fact or event (past and present). It has to do with a word of insight and ability to comprehend concrete facts and situations. It operates sometimes in praying for deliverance for people or events. While in prayer, the person praying will be prompted by the Holy Spirit, who gives insight to someone's need or an event of which the person praying has no prior knowledge. Depending on the situation, there may be a testimony forthcoming that God has performed a miracle. This manifestation is generally in a gathering of the body of Christ for worship and teaching. Some Scriptural examples: Elijah was given insight of 7,000 still true to God (**I Kings 19:18**); Jesus' insight in the heart of Nicodemus (**John 2:25-3:1**) and the woman of Samaria (**John 4: 16-19**)); Jesus saying to the Centurian, "Your son will live" (**John 4:50–53**); and Nathaniel under the fig tree (**John 1:47, 48**).

The Discerning of Spirits *(Diakrisies Pneumaton)*

This gift completes the cycle of the manifestations of revelation everything thing in the realm of knowing a word of wisdom, a word of knowledge, and now the discerning of spirits. The NIV translates this as *"distinguishing between spirits"* whether they be human, divine, or devilish. In others words, this gift or manifestation is not the discerning of evil spirits only, but a discerning of all spirits good or bad. Angels or demons may be seen in some situations. The ability to see or sense the presence or activity of a spirit can only come through the revelation which God gives through the Holy Spirit (i.e., demon possession). It is not a natural judgment, the ability of a person to estimate the qualities of another or psychoanalyze them. It seems that if evil spirits are present, angelic beings and the Holy Spirit will be present also. This manifestation may give insight into the disposition of persons or situations as to good or evil tendencies.

I heard of an experience of the famous evangelist, Aimee Semple McPherson, who discerned demonic spirits surrounding the auditorium in one of her meetings. The atmosphere of the meeting was like a great cloud of depression hanging over the people. She encouraged the audience to start giving praise to God, and as they were lifting up their voices in praise, she discerned angels coming up from behind the demonic figures and standing in front of them. The meeting broke out in spontaneous praise. There were many healing miracles that night. She then told them what she saw. I can't validate this experience, but there are situations in Scripture that reveal the manifestation of this gift. The prophet Isaiah saw the Lord, high and lifted up **(Isaiah 6)**, Elijah prayed that the young man's eyes would be open to see the heavenly armies **(II Kings 6:17)**, Stephen saw heaven open and Jesus standing **(Acts 7:54)**, Peter discerned the motive of Simon, the sorcerer **(Acts 8:20-23)**, and Paul discerned a woman with the spirit of divination **(Acts 16:16–18)**.

The Manifesting Gifts of Power

We now come to those gifts that demonstrate the miraculous power of God. These particular gifts coincide with office gifts and are very important for the work of the ministry. These were demonstrated by Jesus and later early church that served as signs of God's authenticity in the body of Christ.

The Manifestation of Faith *(Pistis)*

Pistis is the ordinary Greek word for faith. However, it is being used here in a different sense. It is said to be given one and not another **(I Corinthians 12:9)**. We must recognize, first of all, that there are other kinds of faith. There is a kind of faith we call natural faith that human beings have for example, the faith of a farmer when he plants seed with the faith that seed will die and burst open, come up out of ground as a simple blade, and grow to a healthy stalk that will produce more corn. In the spiritual realm, there is a kind of faith we call saving faith. A person hears the **gospel** of Jesus Christ, believes it, accepts Jesus into his heart, and is saved. Sometimes this gift of faith mentioned here in I Corinthians is mistaken for the simple or ordinary faith it takes for salvation. This is entirely separate faith from the faith of salvation. This is a special faith that is supernaturally given by God through the Holy Spirit that comes suddenly and fully and performs exploits that cannot be humanly explained. It is a special ability to discern and trust with extraordinary confidence to believe God can and will do the impossible. It is, in a sense, a spontaneous faith that rises to the moment of need. It operates in the experience of the possessor, which enables him or her to sustain unwavering trust in God for divine protection and provision. Some scriptural and other examples would be: Daniel in the lion's den **(Daniel 6)**; the three Hebrew children in the fiery furnace **(Daniel 3)**; Jesus in the temptation **(Luke 4)**; the martyrs' faith throughout history; George Muller, noted English evangelist, who opened an orphanage in his home on a strict faith basis, for which God supplied miraculously, food, clothing, and other needs without fail.

The Manifestation of the Working of Miracles (Energemata Dunameon)

This often confused with the gifts of healing. Healing, for the most part, is a process and may require extended faith and trust. Miracles are generally instantaneous. Miracles are the supernatural demonstration of the power of God by which the very laws of nature are altered, suspended, or controlled. Miracles are used as a sign of the presence of God. They also serve as credentials of divine authority. The apostle John uses the term **"sign(s)"** in his gospel to point to Jesus as the Son of God. **John 20:30, 31** says, *"Jesus did many other miraculous signs in the presence of his disciples which are not recorded in this book. But these are written that you may believe that Jesus is the Christ, the Son of God, and that by believing you may have life in his name."*

Some Scriptural examples are: Elijah on Mount Carmel (**I Kings 18:16**), Moses and the Red Sea (**Exodus 13, 14**), Joshua and Jericho, (**Joshua 5–6**), Jesus calming the storm (**Mark 4:35**), the feeding of the five thousand (**Mark 6:30**), and Jesus raising Lazarus from the dead (**John 11**).

Manifestation of the Gifts of Healing *(Charismata Iamaton)*

Both Greek words are in the plural and should read **"gifts of healings."** This gift is mentioned three times in **I Corinthians 12:9, 28, 30**. It is not certain why the plural is used, but is appears to be used because of the various ways of administering healing to the sick. **Matthew 4:24** says, *"News about Him spread all over Syria, and people brought to Him all who were ill with various diseases, those suffering severe pain, the demon possessed, the epileptics and the paralytics, and He healed them."*

It is basically the supernatural healing of diseases and infirmities without natural means. However, all healing is from God—whether by medicine or doctors who have wisdom from God. In our scientific age, it is common to reject the possibility of God's healing the sick. The church today, in many circles, unfortunately also rejects the possibility, due to its concept that it was only for the time of Jesus and the apostles to authenticate their ministries. The power to heal the sick never resides in a human being. These gifts belong to the Holy Spirit, who manifests them through us, but we never possess them. They always rest upon the power and sovereignty of God, not some so-called "divine healers" or "faith healers" who are mere instruments through whom God applies His power. There are many ways mentioned in Scripture as to how healing is supplied: laying on of hands (**Mark 16:18**), anointing with oil, (**Mark 6:13, James 5:14**), the spoken word (**Matthew 8:8**), applying fabric (**Acts 19:11, 12**), and a shadow (**Acts 5:16**).

The Manifesting Gifts of Inspiration or the Voice of God

We come now to the most controversial section of the vocal **spiritual gifts**. There have been a number of volumes written on the gifts; however, when they come to this section, it becomes obvious to me that they are written without any personal experience of these gifts or at least have only a minimal amount. I came to a personal experience with Christ in Foursquare Gospel Church, which was a somewhat moderate Pentecostal church in the sense they were cautious of the extreme manifestations. I had no prior background to the Pentecostal faith, and I questioned much of their doctrine, especially in terms of the exercise of the gifts of the Spirit. I would like you, the reader, to understand that I am writing as one who became a disciple of the Holy Spirit, searched the Scriptures, and weighed carefully my experiences with the Word of God. This does not infer that I have total understanding, but what I learned and experienced afforded me a fulfilling and rewarding Christian life and ministry. Through the years, I have been grieved by the fact that most churches and congregations have little or no knowledge of these gifts, and in many cases, are not interested in or skeptical of them. I certainly understand the abuse as well as the divisiveness that has occurred in congregations as the result of overzealous, insensitive persons who demonstrate more zeal than wisdom. Certainly the apostle Paul witnessed this in Corinth and possibly other churches. Paul's corrective approach in love in that situation has given encouragement to us. I pray these wonderful gifts will begin to be demonstrated in the body of Christ in these last days. Let us now continue to explore these gifts of inspiration: prophecy, tongues, and the interpretation of tongues. Unlike the gifts of revelation and the gifts of power, these are not the kind that change the world. The gifts of inspiration are strictly for the benefit of the church. They have a three-fold ministry: edification, exhortation, and comfort **(I Corinthians 14:1–5)**. God's desire is that His people would be strong and mature in spiritual matters, as well as alive and powerful. These particular gifts were designed for that purpose.

The Gift of Prophecy *(Propheteia)*

The gift of prophecy here is different than the motivating gift in **Romans 12:6** in that it is an inspired utterance prompted by the Holy Spirit; however, it is not revelatory, nor is it foretelling the future. The motivating gift of **Romans 12** is the ability to verbalize truth (in love), as it were sanctified criticism, constructive in nature and sometimes confrontational. It is not predictive in nature but is akin to preaching. It is unlike preaching, which requires preparation and study. This prophecy is spontaneous, and its purpose is to edify (build up), exhort (instruct), and comfort (encourage) **(I Corinthians 14:3)**. Prophecy seems to be the greatest of the three gifts of inspiration. In **I Corinthians 11–14**, the gift of prophecy is referred to a total of twenty-two times, which seems to indicate its importance. In its expression, it is equal to tongues and interpretation. Paul states that he would like everyone to speak in tongues, but he felt that prophecy would be more profitable for clearer understanding. A message in tongues would require interpretation in order to edify the whole church, wherein prophecy would be more direct. Paul was concerned about the confusion that had already resulted in the misuse of tongues in the Corinthian church. The gift of prophecy is not giving forth any new revelation or truth, but affirming the credibility of truth already known and expressed.

The Exercise and Setting for Prophecy

Paul gives much attention to this gift in **I Corinthians 14,** along with the exercise of the gift of tongues. Both of these gifts and their operation were normally used when people gathered together for worship. In the exercise of these gifts, love must always be the motive **(I Corinthians 14:1)**. Paul gave definite instructions as to how these gifts should operate and bring the church to an orderly, effective ministry. The gift of prophecy in this setting is not confined to appointed prophets, as mentioned in **Ephesians 4:11**, but is more of a ministry of prophecy. In other words, in this type, it is more widely demonstrated throughout Old and New Testaments. For example, we have the **Song of Moses** in **Exodus 15,** which was inspired prophecy directed completely to the praise of God for His saving presence, protection, and establishment of His people.

No doubt it also edified and comforted Israel. We also have the praise of Hannah in **I Samuel 2** in response to God answering her petition for a child she named Samuel, which means *"asked of God."* Her beautiful song of praise provided a model for Mary in the New Testament in her inspired prophetic song **(the Magnificat)** by the Holy Spirit, which recognized the miraculous conception of Christ in her womb **(Luke 1:46–55)**. This was preceded by the prophetic utterance of Elizabeth, her cousin and mother of John the Baptist, prompted by the Holy Spirit as her son, John, leaped in her womb **(Luke 1:41–43)**. As we come to the Day of Pentecost, we witness the apostle Peter standing before three thousand or more people and declaring the miracle of the Holy Spirit, evidenced by the 120 disciples appearing outside the upper room and speaking in tongues and the people hearing these Galileans speaking forth in the various dialects the praises of God. Peter made the following discourse, which announced the ongoing ministry of prophesying. Peter declared to the questioning crowd, asking, "What does this mean?"

Peter replied, *"This is what was spoken by the prophet Joel: 'In the last days,' God says, 'I will pour out my Spirit on all people. your sons and daughters will prophesy, your young men will see visions your old men will dream dreams. Even on my servants, both men and women, I will pour out my Spirit in those days, and they will prophesy'"* (Acts 2:16–18, NIV).

In **Acts 21:7–9**, Paul visited the home of Philip, the evangelist, and discovered Philip's four unmarried daughters who prophesied, who were possibly teenagers. They had a ministry of edifying the church, but they did not foretell the future. The prophetic office always predicts the future; the gift of prophecy never predicts the future. As we mentioned earlier, the ministry gift of prophecy is for edification, exhortation, and comfort. Let's take moment to clarify these threefold purpose of prophesy. It is important that we understand that this prophecy is a divine disclosure on behalf of the Holy Spirit. It is an edifying revelation of the Spirit for a particular moment, a sudden insight of the Spirit, prompting exhortation or comfort.

The first purpose of prophecy is edification. To **edify** means "to build up." This gift will build up those in the body of Christ. The Holy Spirit will prompt a person for a particular moment in the midst of the church to prophesy, and the message may be for those who are fearful or discouraged to edify them to trust God's strength and power. It's the Spirit's means of imparting spiritual strength to be more effective to serve God and the church.

The second purpose is exhortation. In *exhortation,* we have a call to encouragement. I have had the privilege to be part of a congregation where these inspirational gifts were manifested from time to time in the service. I heard words of prophecy exhorting with warning or rebuke, such as the need to be holy, examine one's life, or that Jesus is coming soon and to be alert. This reinforces the Word of God being preached.

The third purpose is that of comfort. For one reason or another, there are many sad people in our congregations. They tend to hide their feelings from fellow Christians because of pride or lest they be seen as weak Christians. People today do not necessarily need sympathy or pity; they need comfort. That's why we need these inspirational gifts operating in our midst. We should be reminded that one of the terms used of the Holy Spirit is **"comforter"** *(parakletos: "one who is called alongside"* **John 14:16, 26)**. The ministry of prophecy comes forth by the prompting of the Holy Spirit, who brings a message of comfort. For example, *"The Lord knows your sorrow and discouragement and distress. 'Be of good cheer; I am with you,' declares the Lord."* This gift is available not to just a few, but the total church. However, within the fellowship of believers, we should always be alert to minister to and comfort one another maybe with just a hand shake and smile, followed by a "God bless you" and "If there is any way I can help you, do not hesitate to contact me. Be assured, I will hold you up in prayer." This may be followed up later with an inquiry by phone.

Paul's Directives for the Manifestation of the Gift

Because this gift of prophecy is possessed by a number of people, the apostle Paul gave some directives to avoid confusion and misuse. First, **I Corinthians 14:32** says that the possessor of the gift of prophecy can control that gift. *"The spirits of the prophets are subject to the prophets."* At times I have had to admonish a person giving an utterance that was out of order for that moment, either because it broke into the sermon being preached or because it created confusion. Unfortunately, the person accused me of "quenching the Spirit." However, the Holy Spirit is very sensitive and a perfect gentleman. The person claimed, "I couldn't control it." First of all, they did not realize that at no time is a person bound by the manifestation of a spiritual gift. The prophet can wait to give the message at the proper moment. That's the difference between being controlled by the devil and being controlled by God. You work with God and discern when it is right and proper to speak. Secondly, prophecies should be restricted to two or three at any one time **(I Corinthians 14:29)**. This avoids confusion, and Paul states, "For God is not a God of disorder but for peace **(I Corinthians 14:33)**. It is perfectly acceptable to have enthusiastic praise and prayers accompanied with clapping of hands or raising hands in praise and singing. However, it generally is done in consensus as a congregation and with the avoidance of unnecessary fleshly demonstrations that would tend not to glorify God. Unfortunately, many churches are fearful and skeptical of allowing such a gift to be part of their worship. If the Scriptural pattern is followed and proper teaching of the gifts is instituted, there should be no fear of unusual fanaticism. What a blessing to have access to these inspirational gifts that can minister edification, exhortation, and comfort to the body of believers in addition to the preaching of the Word of God.

The Gift of Different Kinds of Tongues
(I Corinthians 12:10)

Much has been written concerning the gift of tongues both critical and constructive. Yet with it all there remains a vague idea among Christians as to its true nature. Most commentators are content to explain it as a miraculous power conferred upon the apostles in order to preach the gospel to all nations in their own respective languages. Such an explanation, I believe, disagrees with the plainly recorded facts of the New Testament. The greater problem concerning tongues is due to the fact that it is singled out from the holistic understanding of the person and ministry of the Holy Spirit. Along with this, it is judged by its misuse, witnessed in the immature and insensitive believers, who in most cases, lack the knowledge and purpose of tongues. Another argument about tongues that is readily used to discredit its authenticity is that the phenomenon of tongues appears in other types of religions and cults that are not part of the mainstream of biblical Christianity. How, then, can we explain this? Does it destroy the credibility of the Bible and the Christian experience? Absolutely not! There is rarely a doctrine that doesn't have its counterpart in other religions or cults. For example, the practice of baptism has been found in various forms in other religions and even pagan rituals. Does this nullify baptism used in the biblical context? Not at all. Even the doctrine of communion is found being practiced in some form among a number of religious systems. Does this minimize the Biblical practice? The answer to all these is no! What one will discover is that for every counterfeit, there must be an original. Satan has always distorted and tried to duplicate God's work and bring confusion and doubt. We have a classic example within the Old Testament in Exodus when the wise men, sorcerers, and Egyptian magicians were able to duplicate what Moses and Aaron did before Pharaoh. Because Pharaoh's magicians could duplicate the acts of Moses and Aaron, his heart was hardened, and he refused to let the people of Israel leave Egypt. However, it should be noted that God always intervened and counteracted their false deeds **(Exodus 7–11)**.

One of the great principles I have learned from Scripture is that rather than fighting false teachings or actions, one should put greater effort in teaching the truth of Scripture, thus counteracting the false and strengthening others in the truth. The desire to understand the manifestation of tongues came early in my Christian experience. It was a frequent manifestation in the church I attended and experienced salvation. I was very troubled about it and would ask a number of people in the church who exercised this gift if they could explain it to me. Some were embarrassed because they couldn't explain it adequately but directed me to several Scriptures concerning it. I was encouraged to pray and simply ask God to baptize me with the Holy Spirit. I would pray but then get fearful of what would happen to me. Several well-meaning believers would invite me to pray with them at the altar. They encouraged me to start praising fervently. This didn't help because of my timidity and fear of drawing attention to myself. They continued to help me by "speaking in tongues" in my ears and urging me to repeat what I was hearing. Then, in desperation, they would have me stand and hold up my arms and have me praise God while they were shaking me and praising with me. I became frustrated and angry and yelled out, "If this is how to receive the Holy Spirit, I'm sorry, I've had enough! Just leave me alone!"About that time, the pastor approached the situation and admonished everyone to leave me alone. The pastor apologized and said, "George, just continue to seek God in your own way and time, and let Him do what He desires in His time." It was about two weeks later that the church had a visiting evangelist who was to give a series of messages concerning the Holy Spirit. His first service was on Sunday evening, and his message was, ***"Stephen, a Man Full of the Holy Spirit"*** from **Acts 6:8**. I was intrigued by his message as he emphasized the boldness that Stephen demonstrated under the power of the Holy Spirit—even to the moment of his being stoned to death (**Acts 7:54–60**). This is what I was looking for, to be bold for Christ. I realized that it wasn't a matter of whether I spoke in tongues or not, but that I needed the Holy Spirit's power or ability to be a witness. That's what **Acts 1:8** revealed: ***"But you shall receive power, when the Holy Spirit comes on you; and you will be my witnesses."***

The evangelist gave an invitation to those who would desire to receive this power to come forward to the altar. A number of people went forward, and I joined them as we stood with our eyes closed and praying. The evangelist proceeded to pray with each one, and when he came to me and placed his hand on my head, suddenly I experienced strong presence of God, and I began to speak in tongues! I had such a sense of joy and power, I began to walk around the church auditorium, embracing people and speaking in tongues, crying, laughing, and praising God in English as well as in tongues. I knew at that moment that I had been empowered by the Spirit.

As the evening service ended, I proceeded to my car to go to my job, working the night shift at a plastic factory a few miles from the church. I arrived early, so I remained in the car and began reflecting on my experience when again I sensed the presence of the Lord, and again I began to speak in tongues. The Holy Spirit filled my heart with joy, and I cried, laughed, and praised God. I looked at my watch and discovered I was almost late for work. The nature of the job required that the workers take short, staggered breaks about every three hours. There were approximately twenty to twenty-five workers on this shift, and that night, because I had experienced boldness that I never had before, I was able witness about Jesus to every one of those workers by the end of the shift! I have taken time to testify of this experience because I learned some very valuable lessons about what it means to be a true disciple of Jesus Christ and a disciple of the Holy Spirit under the authority of Jesus Christ. I learned that it is important not to merely seek an experience, but to surrender your will and desire to the person of Jesus Christ; one cannot force an experience upon another person or manipulate the gifts of the Holy Spirit; and it is important that we understand our motives for receiving God's gifts. My motive was to have boldness in my life to give unashamed witness Christ. We must realize the Holy Spirit is a person and not some mystical unexplainable experience. The Word of God must be the foundation of our discipleship so our thoughts and actions can be obeyed without fear and give glory to God.

I received the baptism of the Holy Spirit in 1950. My life was transformed. Even though I was born again and had assurance of salvation, I was lacking empowerment in serving Christ. I was introverted, timid, and had a difficult time conversing and enjoying fellowship with people. The Holy Spirit opened up a whole new dynamic relationship with the Lord. God called me into the ministry, and I thought surely He made a mistake, but through the power of the Holy Spirit, my love for the Lord, and His mission to the world, I was challenged to go forward. My life today is full of memories of how He has used me and is still using me in my latter years. This would not have been possible without the work of the Holy Spirit in my life. Let us now continue to explore what the Word of God has to say about the gift of tongues given by the Holy Spirit for every believer in the body of Christ.

The Manifestation of Tongues on the Day of Pentecost (Acts 2)

Jerusalem was filled with joyful, excited people. This was the time of the great Jewish festival of Pentecost. This was celebrated fifty days after the feast of unleavened bread and was also associated with the Passover **(Exodus 24:22; Deuteronomy 16:10)**. After the exile, it became one of the great pilgrimage feasts of Judaism, and many of those who lived in remote sections of the Roman world returned to Jerusalem for worship. For example, *"Paul had decided to sail past Ephesus to avoid spending* *time in the province of Asia, for he was in a hurry to reach Jerusalem, if possible, by the day of Pentecost"* (**Acts 20:16**). Most people only know Pentecost as a Christian holiday that commemorates the day when the Holy Spirit fell on the apostles and disciples of Christ as they gathered in the upper room after the ascension. While the apostles and disciples remained in Jerusalem out of obedience to Christ (**Acts 1:4–5**), the Scriptures tell us that Jews from many different nations were also present (**Acts 2:5, 9–11**). They were there for a different reason the Jewish feast of Pentecost.

To the Jewish people, Pentecost has historical and agricultural significance. Historically, Pentecost commemorates the giving of the Torah *(the Law)* to Moses on Mt. Sinai. Since God accommodated His Law to an agricultural people, it imposed upon the Jews various grain offerings. So, agriculturally, Pentecost also commemorated the time when the first fruits of the wheat harvest were harvested and brought to the temple in the form of two cakes of unleavened bread (Leviticus 23:17). As Christians, we may ask ourselves what significance there is to the fact that Jesus decided to pour out His Holy Spirit upon the Church on this Jewish feast. I think there are some instances in which the Christian celebration of Pentecost proves to be a sort of fulfillment of the significance of the Jewish feast. The Jewish feast celebrates the beginning of the wheat harvest by offering the first of the harvested wheat to the Lord. In the Christian feast, we celebrate the beginning of the Christian church, when Jesus harvested three thousand souls who were cut to the heart by Peter's preaching and were baptized (**Acts 2:14–41**). We, too, are a kind of first fruits by the grace He has given us (**James 1:18**). Finally, the Spirit that the church received on that day guides us into all truth and knowledge of God's will in a way that far surpasses what was given by the Torah. So, in many ways, the Jewish feast of Pentecost was a perfect day to set in motion the Church that God had in mind from the very beginning. When Jesus gave the command: "Do not leave Jerusalem, but wait for the gift my Father promised" (**Acts 1: 4**), I believe He was asking them to stay until the day of Pentecost arrived.

Acts 2:1–4 says, *"When the Day of Pentecost came, they were all together in one place. Suddenly a sound like the blowing of a violent wind came from heaven and filled the whole house where they were sitting. They saw what seemed to be tongues of fire that separated and*

came to rest on each of them. All of them were filled with the Holy Spirit and began to speak in other tongues as the Spirit enabled them." The function of Acts 2 was an inaugural sign to announce the advent of the Holy Spirit and God's worldwide intention. Let us consider some pertinent features concerning these tongues at Pentecost: First of all, the tongues on the day of Pentecost were languages unknown to the speakers but known to the hearers. However, it was not ***preaching in tongues!*** The 120 were not directing their speaking to the crowd—the crowd was overhearing them speaking praises to God, and they heard these praises in their own *dialect* (**Acts 2:6, 8;** the Greek word for **"tongue"** here is ***dialectos)***. Secondly, the disciples were speaking in tongues before the crowd gathered, not because the crowd gathered. They were praising and worshiping God. Thirdly, there is no evidence of preaching in tongues anywhere is Scripture. There are those who still hold on to the idea that the tongues were actual languages given so they could preach around the world in any language to fulfill the great commission of **Matthew 28:18–20**. Fourthly, if was preaching, why did the crowd say to Peter, "What does this mean?" In fact, when Peter answered their question, he stood up and lifted his voice (not speaking in tongues) to them in Greek or possibly Aramaic. There were known languages commonly used at this time namely, Latin, Greek, and Aramaic. There have been times when tongues have been spoken in actual languages, but this has not been a continuous situation.

A missionary friend of mine, while ministering in Japan, was very discouraged due to the lack of converts and was considering returning home from the mission field. During a small prayer meeting, a young Japanese girl began to speak in English and was admonishing the missionary not to leave her ministry. The missionary was amazed, because this Japanese girl did not know or speak English before! Some of the misunderstanding of the manifestation of tongues is due to the fact that there are two basic types of tongues that are manifested among believers. The first is considered a devotional tongue or referred to as a prayer language. This is available to every believer who has been baptized in the Spirit and functions to edify and give added strength to his or her prayers. In **I Corinthians 14:2, 14–16,** we find both the devotional or prayer tongues which are private in nature ("my spirit prays"). There is, however, a manifestation of tongues which is not given to every believer but serves as a congregational tongue accompanied by the gift of interpretation of tongues, which serves to edify the gathered body of Christ. This, then, brings us to consider this last gift mentioned under the inspirational gifts, the gift of interpretation of tongues.

The Gift of Interpretation of Tongues
(I Corinthians 14:5, 13, 27, 28)

This gift is a supernatural revelation through the Holy Spirit which enables the Christian believer to communicate in the language of the listeners the dynamic equivalent of that which was spoken in tongues. Here again, if tongues consisted of the ability to speak a given foreign language, what would be the need for an interpretation? The congregation will remain un-edified by a tongue if there is no interpretation (**I Corinthians 14:28**). The interpreter receives an equivalent of the tongue, not a word-for-word translation. The length of time speaking may not correspond to the time spent over the actual speaking in tongues. Paul gives some points of order concerning the employment of these gifts in the public service. When tongues are legitimately employed, the leader should give time for an interpretation. There should be no competition among interpreters. If anyone speaks in a tongue, two or three at the most should speak, one at a time, and someone must interpret (**I Corinthians 14:27**). If there is no interpreter, the speaker should keep quiet. The reason for these points of order is that God is not the author of disorder, but of peace (**I Corinthians 14:33**). The whole issue of tongues will remain a mystery to most people who will not make the effort to investigate the Scriptures using the proper rules of interpretation for reasonable understanding.

Some years ago, I was asked to conduct a seminar concerning the theology of the Holy Spirit. At the conclusion of the seminar, I gave time for questions and discussion. The prominent question was, "Can you explain the purpose for speaking in tongues, which seems to be nothing more than emotional gibberish?" I was taken back, because I thought that the seminar presentation gave sufficient evidence for the validity of tongues. As I was about to rehearse some of the evidence again, I decided to respond with a question: "Can any of you explain the phenomena of laughter?" There are many expressions of laughter: "Ha-ha," "Ho, Ho,"

"Hee-hee", or a series of snickers. Can we analyze these? We can only say that they are a combination of consonants and vowels that make no sense. We accept laughter, because we know it is part of the human psyche. When someone laughs, we look for the context that is making them laugh. Were they responding to a joke that they heard or something they saw that was funny to them? If we cannot find the context, we presume something may be wrong with them and they need help. You see, though we do not truly understand laughter, we do know what it does for us. It edifies us, sometimes comforts us, and certainly makes us feel good. Even Scripture states, "A cheerful heart is good medicine, but a crushed spirit dries up the bones" **(Proverbs 17:22)**. If we can have this type of phenomena in our human psyche, why is it not believable that God can give us the experience of tongues that is part of our spirit? As it is used in prayer or devotional language to God, though we do not understand it, we know it edifies and comforts us **(I Corinthians 14:2–4, 14, 15)**.

There is a gift of tongues that is given by the Holy Spirit accompanied by interpretation to edify, comfort, and exhort the gathered body of Christ **(I Corinthians 12:10b; 14:13)**. A number of those present at this seminar said that they never thought of it in this way, and they were interested in studying this manifestation of tongues more thoroughly and as objectively as possible. Unfortunately, we tend to analyze things in Scripture through the eyes of prejudice, doubt, and skepticism because they do not line up with our experience. We also tend to filter things through our traditions, and if they don't fit, we refuse to accept them. Even though I had to limit a complete study of the gifts of the Holy Spirit, hopefully the reader will obtain a clearer insight into these gifts and their purpose for the individual believer and the church. I remind you that we need to embrace the fact that we are disciples of the Holy Spirit, seeking to understand that our mission is to practice and proclaim the truth of God to our present generation and make them aware that the kingdom of God is at hand. The gifts of the Holy Spirit are designed to enhance this mission. The motivating gifts, the manifesting gifts, and the office gifts together reveal the holistic work of the Spirit.

The Holistic Work of the Holy Spirit

Motivating Gifts Romans 12	Gifts of the Holy Spirit I Corinthians 12	Office Gifts Ephesians 4:11	Objective
	The Body of Christ		
Prophecy Serving Teaching Giving Organization Mercy	**Gifts of Revelation** (Mind of God) Word of Wisdom Word of Knowledge Discerning Spirit	Prophets Apostles Evangelists Pastors/Teachers	⇑ Perfecting the Saints
	Gifts of Power (Power of God) Faith Gifts of Healing Miracles		⇑ Work of the Ministry
	Gifts of Inspiration (The Voice of God) Prophecy Various Kinds of Tongues Interpretation of Tongues		⇑ Edifying of the Body

Dr. George P. Kimber

Explanation of the Chart of the Holistic Work of the Holy Spirit

It is important that we take time to view how these various gifts work together, revealing the holistic work of the Holy Spirit. Many of our misunderstandings of various issues result in not taking time to look at them in their whole context. Viewing the chart on the previous page, let us begin with the motivational gifts, as seen in **Romans 12:3–8**. As these gifts are distributed and are functioning within the body of Christ, they become a resource for the Holy Spirit to single out individuals as recipients for the operation of the manifesting gifts mentioned in **I Corinthians 12:4–11**. These gifts are given and operated by the Holy Spirit to assure the continued ministry of the resurrected Christ is expressed and verified. They serve to edify (build up), comfort, and exhort the body of Christ. These gifts in their manifestation represent the mind of God, the power of God, and the voice of God. The office gifts of **Ephesians 4:11** are specific offices, appointed by God, designed to assure balance in the operation of the gifts. These offices are for the purpose of equipping the saints for the work of ministry and the edifying or building up of the body of Christ. Therefore, as one views all these gifts as a whole, it should become evident that they all work together that the body of Christ can ultimately bring honor and glory to God.

Chapter Eight

THE INTEGRATION OF THE FRUIT AND THE GIFTS OF THE HOLY SPIRIT

I Corinthians 12:12–31-13:1–13

One of the sad commentaries of the church today is that the true character of the church is misunderstood, and much of our behavior verifies it. **I Corinthians 12:12–31** constitutes one of the most beautiful passages in Scripture concerning the Church, the body of Christ. It was apparent that the Corinthians were unaware of the true character of the Church. I believe this is still a viable testimony of the many congregations today. My experience in expounding the image of the Church as the body of Christ is that it has always been difficult to convince people that it was a legitimate image. Certainly this was the burden that the apostle Paul was carrying as he heard and saw how the Corinthian church had such a misunderstanding of the redemptive work of Christ. It was obvious that they left the message of the cross and began to take the carnal path, which was creating division among them and losing the vision of and desire church unity **(I Corinthians 1:10–17)**. The truths recorded in the Corinthian letter are always being challenged as to their authenticity and effectiveness because of the carnal state of the church. This is especially true of the gifts of the Spirit, especially tongues. I have heard some of my professors in seminary say, "We must be cautious in accepting those things being dealt with in the Corinthian letters because they were a very carnal, troubled church." What we need to remind ourselves is that I Corinthians is a corrective letter and not forbidding or rejecting certain doctrines, but actually correcting their misuse. We appropriate many important truths from the Corinthian letters, such as communion (**I Corinthians 11**), the resurrection (**I Corinthians 15**), stewardship (**I Corinthians 16**), which we dare not take lightly in our evaluation of the worth of these letters.

The Importance of Understanding the Church as the Body of Christ

My image of the church was formed in my childhood, as I attended a large city church with high walls and a towering steeple with bells. The interior had a lofty ceiling with ornate chandeliers and a sanctuary with beautifully polished pews and walls displaying stained glassed windows depicting biblical characters. The front of the sanctuary displayed a rod iron-divided chancel, which contained a section for the choir and a pipe organ. Beyond was a second section that had a large, beautiful altar where the rector conducted the worship. A high pulpit adorned the left corner outside the chancel where the sermon was delivered. I served as an acolyte, assisting the rector in a number of church duties. All of this created a sense of awe and reverence from the moment you entered the church. I have to admit that my sense of this being a holy place requiring reverence was instilled in my heart (with the help of my mother's elbow and stern looks when I was not attentive). Unfortunately, my image of God was that He was untouchable and to be feared. The congregation did not seem to have a sense of fellowship with one another except at church dinners—at least, that was my perception, and I assumed that's what church was all about. I did acquire a respect for the church and religion in this process, but I never had a personal experience of salvation in Christ.

Years later, after being discharged from the United States Navy, taking up residence in California, and becoming married, I was introduced to my in-laws' church. The church was a simple, wood-framed structure and had a plain interior with curtained windows, which reminded me of an oversized house. There were two sections of pews and a platform at the end of the auditorium with an altar railing below and a pulpit above. I questioned,

Disciples of the Holy Spirit

"Is this a church?" As the service began and joyous singing abounded, followed by prayer and personal testimonies, and biblical preaching with congregational responses, I started to realize for the first time that church was not the building; it was the gathering of people worshiping together, being aware of a loving God in their midst. It was in this church setting that I eventually found Christ as my Savior, and I became part of the body of Christ whenever they gathered on Sunday or other occasions. I realized that one cannot simply function alone without the support and love of other believers in the body of Christ. The passage under consideration, **I Corinthians 12:13–31,** is a very significant one in dealing with the character, function, and purpose of the church. Colin Kruse, in ***New Testament Models for Ministry***, says, ***"Paul is trying to deal with the problem of enthusiastic individualism which threatens to bring about the disintegration of the Christian community at Corinth …. What Paul wants to stress is the corporate character of the Christian experience of the Spirit" (117).***

Paul's analogy between the human body and the church is a very apt illustration. The idea of the church being one body is clearly stated in the following passages: ***"Just as each of us has one body with many members, and these members do not all have the same function, so in Christ we who are many form one body, and each member belongs to all the others"*** (Romans 12:4, 5). ***"For we are member of His body. For this reason a man will leave his father and mother and be united to his wife, and the two will become one flesh. This is a profound mystery –but I am talking about Christ and the church"*** (Ephesians 5:30–32). ***"There is one body and one Spirit just as you were called to one hope when you were called. One Lord, one faith, one baptism; one God and Father of all, who is over all and through all and in all"*** (**Ephesians 4:4**). ***"And he is the head of the body, the church; he is the beginning and the firstborn from among the dead, so that in everything he might have supremacy"*** (Colossians 1:18).

When we examine the inferences of **I Corinthians 12**, some of the obvious lessons are:

1. *A Harmonious Unity* Just as the human body is one organic whole, so is the spiritual body of Christ: ***"The body is a unit, though it is made up of many parts; and though all its parts are many, they form one***

body (I Corinthians 12:12); *"Now you are the body of Christ, and each one of you is a part of it"* (I Corinthians 12:27).

2. ***Necessary Diversity*** As the human body must manifest itself in many members, so the church needs different gifts and ministries. Therefore, the body illustrates unity in diversity. Let us first be clear on what unity does not mean: it does not mean uniformity. Unity is oneness. Diversity lends strength to any group of people. Unity binds together diverse elements so that, by virtue of its many strengths, the whole becomes greater than the sum of its parts. Uniformity among Christians is not necessarily good. When carried to extremes, it becomes evil. It can be shown that complete uniformity within the church would not enhance its beauty, but rather detract from it. For example, in the interest of uniformity, Rome had adopted one language, Latin, for its services of worship around the world (but this is somewhat changing today). Surely, there is room within the church of Christ for any number of languages. There are three legitimate modes of baptism found within the church immersion in water, pouring on of water, and sprinkling with water. Yet this has divided many churches. Many find difficulty in one mode of worship some cultures are more emotional and reflect it in their worship; some people's makeup is more stoic in nature. Instead of finding fault with each other for this difference, they should hold one another in high esteem. By the same token, diversity (short of sin), instead of detracting from the glory of the church, enhances it. Paul would have us look at the nature of the body of Christ in **(I Corinthians 12:12–14)** expresses both unity and diversity: ***"The body is a unit, though it is made up of many parts; and though all its parts are many, they form one body. So it is with Christ. For we were all baptized by one Spirit into one body whether Jews or Greeks, slave or free—and were all given one Spirit to drink. Now the body is not made up of one part but of many."***

I Corinthians 12:12 says that we are unified in one body, and Paul is so intent on driving home this point of our oneness in the church that he refers to Christ as the church. We can no more separate Christ from His church than we can separate a head from the body and expect it to have any life. Paul continues to deal with this problem of the Corinthians, understanding that the diversity and unity are both necessary within the body. In **I Corinthians 12:14–19**, Paul addresses the apparent problem of some feeling inferior. Notice that in **I Corinthians 12:15–16**, the statement *"I am not part of the body"* is mentioned twice the perception that they, the church body, don't really need me, the individual, or I have nothing to contribute, so they sit back and let others do the work of ministry. Beginning in **I Corinthians 12:20–26**, Paul addresses the opposite problem, which is just as ridiculous and dangerous to the health of the body as the first one. It's the problem of feeling superior to others around us. That is why we must realize that the Holy Spirit indwells the church body, and the gifts belong to Him to distribute them equally when needed. We are channels through which the gifts operate, but we do not possess them. We must avoid saying, "I have the gift of …" No! The gift resides in the Spirit in its fullness and perfection.

3. *Mutual Equality and Interdependence* The New Testament views the church not as an institution, but as an organism. Christ is our invisible head, and we are His visible body on earth. So how is this organic unity achieved? How did we become a part of this body? That's the message of **I Corinthians 12:13: *"We were all baptized by one Spirit." It is our baptism with the one Spirit that makes the church one body.*** This verse makes clear that racial and social diversity does not prevent incorporation into this one body. All have become disciples of the Holy Spirit under Christ's authority as head of the body, His church (**Colossians 1:18**). No member of the human body exists independently for itself; even the least attractive parts are absolutely vital. By the three terms **weaker, less honorable,** and **unpresentable**, Paul refers to those parts of the body which are internally protected by nature or covered by clothing. Even though our presentable parts need no special treatment, God has combined those members that are given greater honor to the parts that lack it, so that there should be no division in the body, but that its parts should have equal concern for each other (**I Corinthians 12:21–26**).

Being baptized into one body by one Spirit means we have, by our conversion, been immersed into the mystical body of Christ by the indwelling of the Holy Spirit. Therefore, Christ dwells in us by the Holy Spirit, by which He will progressively develop the character of Christ in us. This involves the fruit of the Spirit, which is love and all its facets—joy, peace, patience, kindness, goodness, faithfulness, gentleness, and self-control. However, this experience of baptism is that of the Holy Spirit representing Christ in us, while a subsequent experience, which is referred to as the baptism in the Holy Spirit, He represents Himself, empowering the believers for supernatural ministry. This involves the gifts of the Holy Spirit mentioned in **Roman 12:5–8, Ephesians 4:9–14, and I Corinthians 12:1–31**, which were dealt with in earlier chapters of the book. This brings us to one of the primary theses of this book: the importance of the integration of the fruit of the Holy Spirit with the gifts of the Holy Spirit

The Results of the Integration of the Fruit and Gifts of the Holy Spirit

The fruit of the Spirit supplies the ethical principles of behavior to the operation of the gifts of the Spirit. There has always been a tendency to view the fruit of the Holy Spirit as the primary focus in conservative churches, believing it is the only essential work of the Holy Spirit in the Christian life. This is especially true of those who draw a dispensational line separating the miraculous works of Christ in the gospels and the apostolic period from our modern contemporary day. On the other hand, there are those who believe we need more of the supernatural demonstrated in our days. They tend to criticize those who resist having the possibility of emotional demonstrations in their church services. We dare not separate in any way the complete work of the Holy Spirit. I think the Scriptures are very clear that both the fruit of the Spirit and the spiritual gifts are to continue together until the second coming of Christ. **Hebrews 13:8** informs us that *"Jesus Christ is the same yesterday, and today, and forever."* Our world needs this same Jesus Christ today in His character and His deeds even in greater measure than when He ministered in the past. There is an intense need for the Holy Spirit to cultivate the fruit of the Spirit in the believer along with the operation of the gifts of the Spirit so that together, the Church can be a healthy and dynamic church in these last days. In fact, we must consider that the important aspects of the Christian life are both who we are and what we do. There should no contention between who we are and what we do. If the fruit of the Holy Spirit is not active along with His gifts, it will make us ineffective. We are reminded of the word of our Lord in **Matthew 7:22**: *"Many will say to me on that day, 'Lord, Lord, did we not prophesy in your name, and in* *your name drive out demons and perform many miracles?' Then I will tell them plainly, 'I never knew you. Away from me you evildoers!'"* Jesus warns against self-deception, a mere verbal profession of lordship without obedience to the will of God. It is even possible to be a self-deluded person exercising a spectacular ministry, using the authority of Scripture and the name of Jesus without discipleship.

The authentic character of all miracles is to be decided by the character of him who performs them. The church definitely needs to maintain a balance today in a world that has lost its way and balance of life so they can know Christ as the way, the truth, and the life. That is why I have emphasized the need to see ourselves as disciples of the Holy Spirit under the authority of Jesus Christ to bring a greater consciousness of the Holy Spirit's guidance and ministry through us. The early churches of Pentecost were so directed by the Holy Spirit that they were seen as turning the world upside down **(Acts 17:6)**. In actuality, they were setting the world upright unto God by the power of the Holy Spirit.

Chapter Nine

THE NEED FOR LOVE AS BEING THE *MODUS OPERANDI* IN ALL MANIFESTATIONS OF THE SPIRIT
(I Corinthians 13:1–13)

The content and style of this passage has raised questions of its place in the Corinthian letter. The King James Version seems to suggest that a sharp contrast is being made between the love of chapter 13 and the gifts of chapters 12 and 14. It is not a contrast or even a comparison, but a complement. Chapter 13, referred to by some as a "hymn to love" written at a later time and inserted here. For some reason, this so-called "love hymn" has been lifted out of this letter and used separately in many wedding ceremonies over time. Unfortunately, this has caused people not to see its relevance to the theology of the Corinthian letter. One the other hand, there are those who accept its position as a contrast to the operation of the gifts being unnecessary and possibly divisive and should be replaced and seen as a "more excellent" way for the church to pursue its ministry. I don't intend to become too technical, but this transitional situation from **I Corinthians 12:31 to 13:1** is important in understanding what Paul is saying. **In I Corinthians 12:31,** the Greek word *eti* ("yet") is a temporal adverb, meaning a given situation is continuing. The main assertion of **I Corinthians 12:31a**, *"continue to desire earnestly the greater gifts,"* is supported by the explanation of **I Corinthians 12:13b**, *"and with this* *in mind I am going to show you an utterly extraordinary way" (kath huperbole)* (in which gifts ought to be sought and used). Robertson and Plummer put it this way: *"I am going to point out the way which will show you the best gifts and how to used them the principle of subordinating the self to others" (International Critical Commentary, I Corinthians,* **283, 285**). So we see this not as a contrast, but a progressive complement. I was taught in biblical interpretation to always study any text or scriptural portion in its context. This rule has saved me from embarrassing situations in preaching and teaching the Bible.

As I viewed **I Corinthians 12–14**, I envisioned **I Corinthians 12** as one slice of bread and I Corinthians 14 as a second slice of bread, with **I Corinthians 13** as the meat placed between both slices. The "meat" (love) not only gives substance, but pulls everything together! The people are to keep pursuing love and continue to desire earnestly spiritual gifts. We can desire, but the Holy Spirit decides when it is the greatest interest for the church. Before we consider the virtues of love in I Corinthians 13, I like to share how the power of this virtue was demonstrated in my ministry.

I had the privilege of planting a church in California, and God blessed me with a lovely congregation. We believed in the fourfold ministry of Christ as a **Savior** to a sin-cursed, Satan-deceived world; a mighty **baptizer** with the Holy Spirit to a timid, weak-kneed Church; **a healer** and great physician to a sick and dying humanity; and **a coming king of peace** to a world tired of war, strife, greed, hate, and suffering. These were the basic beliefs which indentified us as a Pentecostal church. I considered my ministry as rather moderate as compared to some of the Pentecostal stereotypes most people observe. At times, this was a struggle for me, because certain parishioners thought the congregation should be more demonstrative and assertive with our beliefs.

There was a particular man, Doug, who I admired for his faith and ability to be a spiritual leader in his home and as a deacon in our church. He was strongly committed to praying for those who were sick in the church and in his home with amazing results. However, he had little patience with those who didn't seem to trust God in this way. My wife became afflicted with several tumors in her body. Doug decided that we were should have a special prayer time and pray continuously for my wife's healing. We prayed for several hours, and Doug decided that my wife should claim the victory. My wife agreed, and we returned to our homes, praising God for this victory. My wife was already scheduled to be at the hospital to prepare for the operation. When we returned to the parsonage, my wife said I should call the doctor and cancel the operation, since she was trusting God. I called the doctor and explained why we were canceling the operation. He, being a Christian, said he understood, but he advised me not to cancel, just in case she changed her mind. When I hung up the phone, my wife began to cry and was fearful. She did not want to discourage Doug's faith and the congregation, so she was willing to not go to the hospital. I immediately called the doctor again, and he thought it was imperative that we go ahead with the operation. I took her to the hospital the next morning, with the surgery scheduled the following day. I returned home in the early evening and went over to the church to pray. Doug had a daily habit of stopping by the church to pray on his way home. It was getting dark, and I was kneeling at the altar when the side door opened. I knew it was Doug. He was later than usual. I waited until he knelt to pray at the front pew, and I decided to slip out. I didn't want to deal with him, because I knew he was angry that I had taken my wife to the hospital. As I started to leave, he cried out, "Pastor, I need to talk to you." I wasn't ready for his rebuke, and I was angry that he pressured my wife to risk her life in order to keep from disappointing him. Suddenly, he hugged me and cried, "Pastor, please forgive me!" He said that while he was driving home from work, he was complaining to the Lord, "How can I stay with this church when the pastor and his wife have such little faith for healing and miracles and trusting you!"

He went on to say that at that moment, God spoke to him and said, "Doug, you have great faith for healing, and you are disappointed that Nell, the pastor's wife, did not have faith like you. But Doug, have you considered her other virtues that you neglected to see? What about her love and concern for you, not wanting to disappoint your faith, the joy she brings to the congregation and personally to your family and children, her ministry to the shut-ins and hospital calls?"

Doug said, "Pastor, God humbled me tonight and made me realize that although I have a spiritual gift, I am very weak in demonstrating the fruit of the Spirit in my life." Doug found a new wholeness and his life took on a love and compassion which became evident to all. He became a

Barnabas to me and became my prayer partner on my various visitations and crisis situations. The integration of the fruit of the Spirit with the gift made a difference in Doug's understanding of what it meant to be a true disciple of the Holy Spirit.

The Absolute Necessity of Love to Everything Else (I Corinthians 13:1–3)

Von Harnack speaks of this chapter as ***"the greatest, strongest, deepest thing that Paul ever wrote" (I.C.C., I Corinthians, 286)***. Paul is apparently contrasting the various classes of gifts when he compares their value without love. He chooses representative gifts of speaking (tongues), knowing (prophecy), acting (faith to move mountains), and giving (I give all I possess to the poor) any of these without love has no value. Paul is not referring to just any kind of love; it is ***agape*** love, God's love that is imparted to all believers. Since love is the fruit of the Spirit, Paul is saying that love is the motivation for good relationships and positive action. Love is the way we live. This is the missing ingredient in most charismatic meetings. The character of Christ does not shine through or become the governing factor in the manifestation of the gifts. In other words, it is important that we demonstrate the love of Christ and think how His attitude and actions would be evident in the Corinthian assembly when gifts were being manifested. I can remember a number of incidents where just plain courtesy was missing. I remember one particular time when a group from our church wanted to attend a divine healing meeting in Chicago being conducted by a well-known healing evangelist. As we arrived, hundreds of people were huddled in front of the doors, anxiously waiting for them to open. There were a number of people in wheelchairs; some were on crutches, others had canes, and even a few were lying on cots. When the doors opened, to my surprise and amazement, the crowd burst forth like excited cattle, pushing, shoving, hollering to each other, and actually making it impossible for the sick and afflicted to get through. They scrambled for the front seats in order to be close to the stage and the evangelist. Where were the compassion, love, courtesy, and respect that should have been exercised to help those people who were in desperate need?

As Paul rehearsed this whole concept of love in I Corinthians 13, he stressed that it must be the *modus operandi* in all the manifestations of the Spirit, whether in the exercise of the gifts or in everyday life. He is, in effect, expressing again the fruit of the Spirit previously expounded in **Galatians 5:22, 23**. Spiro Zodhiates states, *"If you were to take I Corinthians 13 to be a commentary on Galatians 5:22, 23, you might very well put a colon after 'love in the enumeration of the fruits of the Spirit, for they truly spring from it'" (I Corinthians 12, Vol. 1, 331).* Let us consider how the integration of the **"love way,"** which is the heart of discipleship, regulates or governs the use of the gifts of the Spirit, which was a major problem in the Corinthian church.

The Characteristics of Love (I Corinthians 13:4–6)

These characteristics should be evident in the life and ministry of the disciples of the Holy Spirit, especially in relation to the operation of the gifts within the community of faith.

"Love is patient" (I Corinthians 13:4a). One should immediately connect this attribute with the fruit in **Galatians 5:22**. Patience is the willingness to wait. William Barclay observes that in the New Testament, the word always speaks of patience with people, not with circumstances ***(Letters to the Corinthians, 133)***. It is longsuffering with those who do not hold one's views of the gifts or those who, through timidity or fear, hesitate to use their gift.

"Love is kind" (I Corinthians 13:4b). Here is love on the active side, looking for a way of being kind and loving to someone. It looks for a way of being constructive. From the description of the way the Corinthians observed their love feasts **(II Corinthians 11:17–22)**, it appears that they were anything but kind to one another. Here again, **Galatians 5:22** refers to kindness as part of the fruit of the Spirit.

"Love does not envy or show jealousy" (I Corinthians 13:4c). One does not envy the more prominent gifts in others. There are two kinds of envy. One is the kind that covets the possessions of other people. The other kind is worse; it resents the very fact that others have what they don't have. Love does not envy those who have a greater following because of their gift. The Corinthians were torn by envy, as seen by the perilous divisions which had split up their congregation into petty cliques. Love could mend schisms in the body **(I Corinthians 12:25)**.

"Love does not boast" (I Corinthians 13:4d). The person who boasts or brags may be speaking the truth, but the glory is directed to the person and not God. William Barclay says that *"true love will always be far more impressed with its own unworthiness than its own merit"* **(Letters to the Corinthians, 134)**.

"Love is not proud (puffed up)" (I Corinthians 13:5). This has to do with exaggeration and sensationalism. This has always been a danger for gifted people. This has been a particularly prominent attitude in the charismatic movement, such as exaggerating the number of people saved, healed, or baptized in the Spirit. There is also a tendency to emphasize how unusual miracles happen as a result of a person sowing seed of so much money to a particular ministry. This is not to say that some of these things do not happen, but they are generally held up as supposedly the norm for charismatic ministries that preach the popular, so-call health-and-wealth gospel.

"Love is not rude" (I Corinthians 13:5a). This can also be stated as *"does not act "unseemly"* **(KJV)**. Paul had to at times speak to the disorderliness of the Corinthians. Everything should be done decently and in order. There is much rudeness displayed in meetings and passed off as the move of the Spirit. This refers to courtesy of politeness and is guided by consideration of the feelings of others. Actually, this was the Greek word ***aschemonei***, referring to the sexual organs, implying that love will not do that which is unpresentable or could not be exposed to public view, that is, it could not behave disgracefully *(**Arndt and Gingrich Greek Lexicon, 118, 119**)*.

"Love is not self-seeking" (I Corinthians 13:5b). Selfishness is the opposite of love. It is possible to seek personal satisfaction in the exercise of the gifts. A Christian may feel unloved or insignificant. But with the discovery of his or her gift and its function in the body of Christ, he or she may appear to be more important in his or her own eyes. This can happen, especially in the exercise of prophecy and speaking in tongues. The whole purpose of these particular gifts is to edify the members of the body of Christ. This is the purpose and concern of the Holy Spirit, who dwells within us and speaks through us. Now Paul refers to love's reaction to the

sins of others due to their attitude toward one another. Since the fruit of the Spirit says love is patient, so Paul points out to the Corinthians that love is not easily angered.

"Love is not easily angered" (I Corinthians 13:5c). There are times when our fellow Christians can create difficult situations toward each other. Sometimes these actions are intentional; other times, they are imagined. This does not mean that we will never get angry at another person, but one does not burst into rage. Love displays patience. If we take time to investigate and think about such actions, we may be able to handle the situation more readily with grace and forgiveness.

"Love keeps no records of wrongs" (I Corinthians 13:5d). It always good to give room to allow people to change and begin new relationships. This certainly directs our attention to the need for forgiveness. I remember how I kept such records against several people who caused me great difficulty in pursuing my theological training. I held that attitude in my heart for a number of years, until one day, when I was rehearsing the situation to my wife, who had heard this over and over again. She said to me, "Honey, you need to destroy this record of wrong and forgive, once and for all." I pursued that admonition and was able to bring forgiveness to the forefront, and it resulted in bringing the fresh air of freedom in my heart and mind. I destroyed those mental records I had been keeping for so long, and I was able to focus and think on those things that are lovely, pure, and praiseworthy **(Philippians 4:8)**. How could I minister by the Holy Spirit if I was grieving Him?

"Love does not delight in evil but rejoices in truth" (I Corinthians 13:6). It doesn't delight in the wickedness of others, as in the Corinthian church where a man was in an incestuous relationship with his stepmother **(I Corinthians 5)**. In fact, they were gloating of their liberty! Love rejoices over truth wherever it is found. Falsehood has become a constant in most of our communities. We delight in news stories of celebrities and prominent people caught in falsehoods of many kind and delight when they escape punishment. Someone said, "A lie can travel around the world before truth can get its shoes on!" Paul concludes this section with some positive actions love performs. Love protects the welfare of others; love always trusts and gives people the benefit of the doubt and gives time for people to prove themselves. Love always hopes, being confident of the God of hope, whose promises never fail. Love perseveres; it never gives up, but endures hardships, persecution, and other troubles, knowing that **"he who endures to the end shall be saved" (Matthew 10:22)**. God still loved the Corinthian church and did not give up on it. The church today needs to take heart as to the power and quality of love from God through the Holy Spirit. Finally, *love never fails!* As we can see by the deliberation, we have made the characteristic of love that Paul knows is the only corrective that will be effective for the Church at large.

Finally, let us observe how the fruit of Galatians 5:22–23 coordinates with I Corinthians 13:1–7 in providing a corrective for the orderly function of the operation of the gifts.

Galatians 5:22–23	I Corinthians 13:1–7
Love	Love does not seek its own; it is not selfish or self-centered.
Joy	Love does not rejoice in iniquity but rather rejoices in the truth.
Peace	Love is not easily provoked, but is serene and stable.
Longsuffering	Love suffers long, perseveres, and is patient.
Kindness (gentleness)	Love is merciful, thoughtful, and concerned; it does not envy.
Goodness	Love is gracious, generous, kind, and good.
Faithfulness	Love thinks no evil but has faith in God and others.
Meekness	Love is humble and gentle; it does not vaunt itself.
Temperance	Love is disciplined, controlled, and does not behave unbecomingly.

The Permanence of Love

"Love never fails. But where there are prophecies, they will cease; where there are tongues, they will be stilled; where there is knowledge, it will pass away. For we know in part and we prophesy in part, but when perfection comes, the imperfect disappears. When I was a child, I

talked like a child, I thought like a child, I reasoned like a child. When I became a man, I put childish ways behind me. Now we see but a poor reflection as in a mirror; then we shall see face to face. Now I know in part; then I shall know fully, even as I am known. And now these three remain: faith, hope and love. But the greatest of these is love" (**I Corinthians 13:8–13**).

These closing verses of this chapter should solidify in our thinking that the fruit of Love will always be the stabilizing factor for disciples of the Spirit and the Church. As long as love is the controlling factor within, the body of Christ can be built up in marvelous ways. It can be a strengthening thing in meeting together, encouraging one another in faith, sharing in the spiritual gifts, being taught by the mind of God and the Spirit of God through the Word of God, and being comforted in times of trial and testing and pressure. This is the purpose for the church getting together. Since the day of Pentecost, the Holy Spirit was sent by God to empower the followers of Jesus Christ to not only follow Him, but to express their spiritual gifts within the context of *agape* love until He comes again. Paul is stressing its absolute permanency. When all the things pass away that we firmly hold to and cherish in this life, love will still remain firm.

As I was contemplating the possibility of remarriage following the death of my first wife, I realized how important love had been in sustaining my life in marriage until death. In God's providence, He brought a lovely, godly woman into my life and a second opportunity of marriage. We both knew the importance of love as being the governing factor. We were led to a portion of Scripture that we adopted for our union: *"Place me like a seal over your heart, like a seal on your arm; for love is stronger than death, its jealousy unyielding as the grave. It burns like blazing fire, like a mighty flame. Many waters cannot quench love, rivers cannot wash it away. If one were to give all the wealth of his house for love, it would be utterly scorned"* (**Song of Songs 8:6–7**). If only the church could grasp this truth of the power, permanency, and completeness of love, it would reflect the divine love and glory of God.

Paul emphasized that even though we function in our Christian faith, there are three elements that afford us the ability to live a holy life before God: faith, hope, and love. However, as great as faith and hope are, love is still the greatest. Faith without love is cold; hope without love is rather grim. William Barclay says, *"Love is the fire which kindles faith and love is the light that turns hope into certainty."* It seems obvious to me that faith will not be needed in eternity, since we will see everything clearly, including seeing God face to face. We will not need hope in eternity, since the hope of heaven is complete. Love will be experienced throughout eternity and will never diminish. When we foster love in all we are and all we do, we will not be surprised to experience it in its fullness in heaven. The integral relationship between I Corinthians 12 and I Corinthians 13 should now be clear to us. I appreciate how this is summarized by Charles Hummel: *"Although Paul's essay on love can stand by itself, perhaps gracing a wedding ceremony, but its message is essential to the exercise of spiritual gifts. It is shaped and created for the very purpose of demonstrating the solution to the tensions in the Corinthian congregation" (Fire in the Fireplace, 147).* The principle of love is also important to I Corinthians 14 as Paul attempts to bring order to the worship service. Paul applies the attributes of love presented in **I Corinthians 13.** Here, it is evident that these were necessary because of the confusion taking place in the operation of the gifts. It is important that unity and harmony be present in the body of Christ in the midst of its unique diversity. God would be glorified, and the church would be strengthened and motivated to minister to its members and the world. An unbelieving world would know that God is real and alive and can meet their need of salvation and hope of eternal life.

The Importance of the Proper Regulation of Spiritual Gifts (I Corinthians 14:1–40)

The manifestation of divine power always attracts some impressionable, but misguided, selfish, or unbalanced persons who cannot or will not submit to scriptural order. Where there is a lack of holistic teaching on the gifts, sincere people often, for lack of such knowledge, react to spiritual operations in a manner that is not in the best interest of the church. It is imperative that people be taught to properly govern themselves under the impression of the Spirit's power, but this is very difficult. I do not want to give the impression that I am opposed to the manifestation of the power of God; neither am I insinuating that the exercise of the gifts will more than likely end in fanaticism or extremes. My observation and experience have been that where there has been proper teaching followed by proper regulations with discernment, fear of fanaticism is dispelled.

The apostle Paul was very concerned that the Corinthians seemed to be taking everything to excess and found it necessary for them to heed his correctives. He began by urging them to "follow the way of love" **(I Corinthians 14:1)**, of which he has expounded so beautifully in **I Corinthians 13**. Whatever gift one may possess, if the love previously set forth by Paul is lacking, such gifts fail to glorify God and bless the body of Christ. I am fully aware of those who advocate that these gifts are to be considered transitory and not permanent and that the exercise of love takes precedence over the gifts. I agree that love certainly is greater than the gifts, but I believe Paul is insisting that the gifts are valid and should be motivated and practiced in love. Submitted to the will of the Holy Spirit, they will be effective in their purpose to edify the community and demonstrate God's love and power (I **Corinthians 14:3–5)**. Having made love the criterion of judgment and value and made it clear that the fruit of the Spirit is available to every member of the community, Paul turned his attention to the two gifts that were being abused, namely, prophecy and tongues. In the process of correcting this situation, Paul spoke the truth in love.

It is not my intent to expound this entire chapter, but I want to point out a few of the significant things that substantiate the thesis of this book, namely, that there must be a proper integration of the fruit of the Spirit with the gifts of the Spirit in order for them to operate properly. Again, let me emphasize that recognizing that we are, as it were, disciples of the Holy Spirit under the authority of Jesus Christ, the exercise of love will always be at the forefront. The answer to the Corinthian issue and to all church problems is to act in love. Here is where the Christians and the Christian community must always begin. Paul proceeded to offer specific correctives to the church of the apparent unbridled use of tongues in the congregation and that they should especially desire to prophesy, as compared to speaking in tongues **(I Corinthians 14:1)**. Although Paul did not prohibit the speaking in tongues, he pointed continually to the need for clarity in communication. Therefore, love would draw one to prophecy rather than speak in tongues for the consideration and benefit for fellow believers (**I Corinthians 14:19**).The apostle would have them observe that he who speaks in tongues speak not to men, but to God. No one will understand him, because in personal prayer (devotional tongues), he speaks mysteries (**I Corinthians 14:2**). However, if one speaks with the gift exercised by the Spirit to the congregation (congregational tongue), it would be followed by the gift of interpretation thus, the church would receive edification. Not everyone has the congregational gift of tongues, so there must be discernment as to which type of tongues is being exercised (**I Corinthians 14:1–4**). The main issue between tongues and prophecy is that of ***intelligibility***. Therefore, the gift of prophecy is preferred, because it is addressed to the people precisely for their edification (**I Corinthians 14:3**), and in that sense, it is the greater gift. Since the various ministries are to be done for the edification of the church, Paul continues to show how this may be accomplished for tongues and prophecy, especially in the exercise of tongues. Three guidelines are given in **I Corinthians 14:27**. Subsequently, the number of prophecies is to be limited at any one time in the service (**I Corinthians 14:29**). The divine gift of prophetic utterance is put under the control and responsibility of the possessor (**I Corinthians 14:32**), even though the message is given by the Holy Spirit.

I have encountered personal rebuke when I questioned the expression of such gifts both tongues and prophecy being exercised in a disorderly manner thus accusing me of hindering or grieving the Holy Spirit. I would remind them that they have the responsibility as to when to deliver their message, discerning whether it would simply disrupt the service or bring proper edification to the community (**I Corinthians 14:26–30**). Most of the time, they are unaware that it is under their control. I recall a situation that occurred while I attended a conference where my pastor was the keynote speaker. While he was delivering his message, suddenly a message in tongues came forth from the congregation. My pastor paused and waited for a possible interpretation to come forth, but none came, so he continued with his sermon. I remember my confusion as to why there was no interpretation if the message in tongues was given by the Holy Spirit. As my pastor ended his sermon, a fellow minister, who had been seated behind him on the platform, stepped up to the microphone and explained why there was no interpretation given. He said, "I had the interpretation, but I felt retrained to give it, and I wasn't quite sure why. But when the pastor resumed his sermon, to my surprise, the next words he spoke were the exact words I had received from the Holy Spirit. Then I realized that my message was not needed at that time and could have created confusion." This substantiates that fact that "God is not the author of confusion but of peace" **(I Corinthians 14:33)**. I am convinced if we would recognize that we are to be disciples of the Holy Spirit which is indwelling us and producing the character of Christ, evidenced by the fruit of the Spirit, there would not be the confusion and misunderstanding of the purpose and ministering of the gifts of the Spirit. We need to take a fresh look at the life and ministry of the Holy Spirit in the days we have left before the coming of our Lord Jesus Christ.

Chapter Ten

DISCIPLES OF THE HOLY SPIRIT TODAY AND BEYOND

Rethinking the Importance of Recognizing Ourselves as Disciples of the Holy Spirit

My concept of disciples of the Holy Spirit is not replacing our being disciples of Jesus Christ, but rather identifying our relationship as relevant to the church age. When we think of ourselves as disciples of Christ, it could be conceived as merely being followers of the Jesus of the ancient past, learning from Him and imitating Him, but without the indwelling power of the Holy Spirit. The resurrection brought a new perspective for His disciples and future disciples. It is not a matter of merely imitating Him, but being empowered by Him. It allows Christ to be ever-present through the life and ministry of the disciples of the Holy Spirit. The disciples of the Holy Spirit make up the church as the body of Christ in the present age. The image of the Church as a body has challenged our thinking and has given us directives as to what the life and growth and purpose of the Church should be. It has been observed that *"Christianity began in Palestine with a man, moved to Greece and became a philosophy; to Rome and became an institution; to Europe and became a culture and finally to America, where it became a corporation!"(source unknown).* A return to God's original model for the body of Christ will change the complexion of the Church that, in most cases, has been institutionalized today and has moved toward individualism. The church, in its struggle to be relevant and contemporary, has allowed the culture to dictate what the church should be and do. The church today is divided over many matters, such as the forms of worship, types of buildings, what dress code is acceptable, the relevance of exegetical Biblical preaching over more informal styles, the inerrancy of the Bible, and numerous other innovations. It is time for the Church to get back to the commission *"to be disciples and make disciples"* **(Matthew 28:18–20)**.

I am suggesting that we need to be disciples of the Holy Spirit as the body of Christ. If we are disciples of the Holy Spirit, indwelling and shaping the body of Christ, what should the Church look like? Just as the Holy Spirit builds us into the image of Christ, so collectively He builds Christ's church to reflect His glory. First of all, for this to happen, the church today must turn its focus from seeing only the horizontal realm and begin also to look toward and include the vertical realm. Charles Colson, in his book, ***Being the Body***, mentions Richard Halverson, former pastor of Fourth Presbyterian Church near Washington, DC as saying, *"We need to see the church from a higher perspective. We need the big-picture view of the Body, alive and vibrant, the holy presence in the world. The church's role in the world is not a series of independent items on an action list. Instead, the church's role (what is does) is dependent on its character (what it is) as a community of believers. What we do, therefore, flows from who we are" (311)*. Paul expressed the same idea as to how the church should function: *"Since then, you have been raised in Christ, set your hearts on things above, where Christ is seated at the right hand of God. Set your minds on things above, not on earthly things. For you died, and your life is now hidden with Christ in God. When Christ, who is your life, appears, then you also will appear with him in glory"* **(Colossians 3:1–3)**.

Since Christ is resurrected, the Colossian church was admonished by Paul to establish those things given to them by the Holy Spirit so that the Church may be strong until the coming of Jesus Christ. Paul has reminded his readers that it is in their union with Christ and His power and encouragement that holy living is produced in the world until He comes. It is imperative that the Church function as a body, with Christ as the head and each member being filled with His Holy Spirit, demonstrating the gifts of the Spirit by edifying, exhorting, and comforting the whole body. It is also imperative that each member is endowed with the fruit of the Spirit that will be the governing factor for the healthy operation of the gifts within the body of Christ. If the body of Christ determines to purpose and to obey this holistic paradigm, the church will be powerful and healthy within and be attractive to those who are looking for a church that can show the reality of Christ and meet their earthly and eternal needs.

I am convinced that if we begin to see ourselves as disciples of the Holy Spirit, following the directives of Christ given through the Holy Spirit for us, we can bring honor and glory to God and draw many people into the kingdom of God. The end time has come, Christ is at the threshold of heaven, and the shout of the archangel and the trumpet of God is about to sound. The apostle Peter describes the Day of the Lord and reminds us of our task as disciples of the Holy Spirit and as the body of Christ: in **II Peter 2: 1-13.:**

1. We must be stimulated to wholesome thinking by the Word of God **(1, 2)**.
2. We must be aware of the scoffers who argue against the coming of Christ **(3, 4)**.
3. We must recognized that God's promised future judgment is sure as revealed in the time of Noah **(5–7)**.
4. We must recognize that God is not controlled by our way of thinking of time **(8, 9)**.
5. We must realize that the Day of the Lord will come with horrific results **(10)**.
6. We must evaluate our lives and help others to do so in the light of this great day of destruction **(11, 12)**.
7. We can rejoice that God will create a new heaven and earth where righteousness will dwell **(13)**.

In light of all of this, it is important that the church concentrates on what it means to be the church in the time we have left before Christ comes. I challenge you, the reader, to think seriously about the reality of becoming disciples of the Holy Spirit and help to establish healthy churches based on being the body of Christ as their first priority. When we establish healthy churches, evidenced by the fruit of the Spirit and integrated with the gifts of the Spirit, people will grow spiritually, and the ministry of the Holy Spirit will be working among them. Evangelism and passion for the lost will be the by products and will bring glory to God; many will be prepared for eternity and the glory for heaven. May the admonition to the Church of Philadelphia in **Revelation 3:11, 17** encourage us in these last days: *"I am coming soon. Hold on to what you have, so that no one will take your crown. He who has a ear, let him hear what the Spirit says to the churches."*

DISCUSSION QUESTIONS FOR EACH CHAPTER

Chapter One: Who Is the Holy Spirit?

1. The author refers to several major issues that created confusion concerning the Holy Spirit. Do you agree or disagree? What are some of the issues that have confused you?
2. Discuss how the Scriptures reveal that the Holy Spirit is a person and not just impersonal images being expressed about God.
3. Do you think the author's diagrams give better understanding of the Godhead relationships? Discuss your understanding and questions about the Godhead, especially the role of the Holy Spirit.

Chapter Two: The New Testament Pattern of Holy Spirit Discipleship

1. Discipleship is not exclusive to Christianity, since many cultures had those who sought out their wise men and philosophers to be their disciples. How were disciples of Jesus unique in their discipleship?
2. Why do you think discipleship is important to Christianity and the church today?
3. How can a discipleship program be developed in your church or small groups?

4. Do you think the author's premise for designating believers today as disciples of the Holy Spirit has merit? If not, then why?

Chapter Three: Jesus, the Unique Model of Holy Spirit Discipleship

1. What are the implications of the Scriptural concept of Jesus being the God-man?
2. How does Jesus portray or model discipleship? Give examples.
3. In what way does Mark's gospel account serve as the basis for the pattern of discipleship?

Chapter Four: The Ethical Foundation for Disciples of the Holy Spirit

1. Choose one or two beatitudes and discuss their ethical implications in regard to the operation of the spiritual gifts within the church.
2. Discuss some of the examples of how the apostle Paul, Peter, and James express the ethical principles of the Beatitudes in their writings.
3. Note how the epistle of James uses the framework of the Sermon on the Mount from Matthew in constructing his letter.

Chapter Five: Disciples of the Holy Spirit: The Fruit Dimension

1. What does it mean to walk (live) in the flesh (desires of the sinful nature) in contrast to the fruit of the Spirit? (Note: ***desires*** is plural; ***fruit*** is singular.)
2. The author divides the categories of the fruit of the Spirit into three groups to better understand how our life in the Spirit is expressed.

3. Discuss the virtues of faithfulness, meekness and self-control in your personal life in the light of today's ever-increasing cultural deterioration and pressures.

Chapter Six: Disciples of the Holy Spirit: The Gifts Dimension

Review the chart comparing the Old Testament prophetic structure as it is reflected in the New Testament structure of the Gifts of the Holy Spirit. Discuss how it reveals the inspiration and unity of the Old Testament with the New Testament.

1. Motivational Gifts (**Romans 12:3–8**)

Identify the various motivational gifts in your congregation and how they are operating. Do you recognize any of these gifts in yourself? Discuss how they might be stimulated and organized in your congregation.

Consider using the drawings of the motivational gifts as a presentation to your Sunday School class or cell group to better clarify its operation.

2. Office or Ministry Gifts/Gifted Leaders (**Ephesians 4:11–16**)

Can we justify the offices of apostles and prophets in the church today? Why or why not?

In Acts, the ministry Philip is in seems to give us the pattern of the ministry of the evangelist. Is this evident today? Why are there so few who consider themselves as specifically called to be evangelists in the church today?

The office gift of pastor/teacher appears to have shepherding skills as well as the task of teaching and equipping the saints. Discuss and react to the diagram of Ephesians 4:11–13.

Chapter Seven: The Manifesting Gifts (I Corinthians 12, 14)

1. What was the basic Corinthian problem, according to the apostle Paul?
2. Discuss why it is important to follow biblical mandates when dealing with the gifts of the Holy Spirit.
3. Do you think the three guiding principles are helpful for people to understand a true manifestation of the Holy Spirit?
4. Discuss how the manifesting gifts contribute toward building a healthy church.

Chapter Eight: The Integration of the Fruit and Gifts of the Holy Spirit

1. What is the advantage of viewing the church as the body of Christ over other images?
2. Why is there a need for the integration of the fruit of the Spirit with the gifts of the Holy Spirit?

Chapter Nine: The Need for Love Being the *Modus Operandi* in all Manifestations of the Spirit (I Corinthians 13:1–13)

1. What is the significance of the "more excellent way" expressed by Paul?
2. Why is love an absolute necessity to everything else in the ministry of the gifts?
3. Choose several characteristics of love and explain their importance to the gifts.

Chapter Ten: Disciples of the Holy Spirit—Today And Beyond

Discuss why there should be a rethinking of the ministry of the Holy Spirit today. How has this book helped you to understand the Holy Spirit? Do you consider the concept of seeing ourselves as disciples of the Holy Spirit is a feasible way to think?

RESOURCES

Betterson, Henry. ***Documents of the Christian Church***. New York: Oxford University Press, 1963.

Bilezikian, Gilbert. ***Community 101***. Grand Rapids, MI: 1977.

Bittlinger, Arnold. ***Gifts and Graces***. Grand Rapids: William B. Eerdmans Publishing Company, 1974.

Bonhoeffer, Dietrich. ***The Cost of Disciplship***. New York: Macmillian Publishing Co., 1963.

Brumback, Carl. ***What Meaneth This?*** Springfield, MO: The Gospel Publishing House, 1947.

Bruner, Frederick Dale. ***A Theology of the Holy Spirit***. Grand Rapids: William B. Erdmans Publishing Company, 1970.

Carter, Charles W. ***The Person and Work of the Holy Spirit: A Wesleyan Perspective***. Grand Rapids: Baker Book House, 1974.

Chambers, Oswald. ***My Upmost for the Highest***. Uhrichsville, OH: Barbour Publishers.

Drescher, John M. ***Doing What Comes Spiritually***. Scottsdale, PA: Herald Press, 1993.

Deer, Jack. ***Surprised by the Power of the Spirit***. Grand Rapids: Zondervan Publishers, 1993.

Ewert, David. ***The Holy Spirit in the New Testament***. Scottsdale, PA: Herald Press, 1987.

Fee, Gordon D. ***The First Epistle to the Corinthians***. Grand Rapids: William B. Erdmans Publishing Company, 1987.

_____. ***Paul, the Spirit, and the People of God***. Peabody, MA: Hendrickson Publishers, Inc., 1996.

Hall, Eddy and Gary Morsch. ***When There is No Burning Bush.*** Grand Rapids: Baker Books, 2004.

Horton, Harold. ***Gifts of the Spirit.*** London: Assemblies of God Publishing House, 1949.

Hummel, Charles E. ***Fire in the Fireplace.*** Downers Grove, IL: Intervarsity Press, 1979.

McQuilkin, Robertson. ***Life in the Spirit.*** Nashville, TN: Broadman & Holman Publishers, 2000.

Morgan, G. Campbell. ***The Corinthian Letters of Paul.*** Old Tappan, NJ: Fleming Revell, 1956.

Stott, John R. W. ***Christian Counter-Culture.*** Downers Grove, IL: Intervarsity Press, 1979.

Tinsley, E. J. ***The Imitation of God in Christ.*** London: SCM Press, 1960.

CPSIA information can be obtained at www.ICGtesting.com
265545BV00002B/1/P